Canada Without Armed Forces?

Canada Without Armed Forces?

Edited by Douglas L. Bland

Published for the School of Policy Studies, Queen's University
by McGill-Queen's University Press
Montreal & Kingston • London • Ithaca

National Library of Canada Cataloguing in Publication

Canada without armed forces? / edited by Douglas L. Bland.

Includes bibliographical references.
ISBN 1-55339-037-7 (bound).—ISBN 1-55339-036-9 (pbk.)

    1. Canada—Armed Forces—Operational readiness. 2. Canada—Military policy. 3. Canada—Foreign relations—1945- I. Bland, Douglas L. II. Queen's University (Kingston, Ont.). School of Policy Studies.

UA600.C344 2004   355'.033071   C2004-900920-6

© Copyright 2004

Preface

The Queen's University Defence Management Studies Program (DMSP), established with the support of the Canadian Department of National Defence (DND), is intended to engage the interest and support of scholars, members of the Canadian Armed Forces, public servants, and participants in the defence industry in the examination and teaching of the management of national defence policy and the Canadian Armed Forces. The program has been carefully designed to focus on the development of theories, concepts, and skills required to manage and make decisions within the Canadian defence establishment.

The Chair of the Defence Management Studies Program is located within the School of Policy Studies and is built on Queen's University's strengths in the fields of public policy and administration, strategic studies, management, and law. Among other aspects, the DMSP offers an integrated package of teaching, research, and conferences, all of which are designed to build expertise in the field and to contribute to wider debates within the defence community. An important part of this initiative is to build strong links to DND, the Canadian Armed Forces, industry, other universities, and non-governmental organizations, in Canada and in other countries.

This book was originally published as part of a series of studies, reports, and opinions on defence management in Canada named for Brooke Claxton, Minister of National Defence from 1946 to 1954. Brooke Claxton was the first post-Second World War defence minister and was largely responsible for founding the structure, procedures, and strategies that built Canada's modern armed forces. As defence minister, Claxton unified the separate service ministries into the Department of National Defence; revamped the *National Defence Act*; established the office of Chairman, Chiefs of Staff Committee, the first step toward a single Chief of Defence Staff; organized the Defence Research Board; and led defence policy through the great defence rebuilding program of the 1950s, the Korean War, the formation of NATO, and the deployment of forces overseas in peacetime. Claxton was unique in Canadian defence politics: he was active, inventive, competent, and wise.

A COOPERATIVE RESEARCH PROJECT

Defence policy generally and force development in particular are complex matters of public policy and administration. This work required the active participation of several expert researchers, administrators, and others from inside and outside government, who contributed to our understanding of the predictable state of the Canadian Armed Forces in the near future. The project, however, was conceived, sponsored, and directed – and this book was produced – as part of the ongoing Defence Management Studies Program. The editor, of course, accepts willingly responsibility for the conclusions expressed in this summary of this extensive research project.

Besides the editor, three scholars widely experienced and currently working on issues directly related to the main themes of this research project were invited to add their recent research findings to this monograph. Brian MacDonald is President of Strategic Insight Planning and Communications. A prominent Canadian media commentator on security and defence issues and the author of numerous studies on Canadian defence policy and administration, he is a graduate of The Royal Military College and York University and author of *Military Spending in Developing Countries: How Much Is Too Much.* Christopher Ankersen served in the Canadian Armed Forces for 12 years as an infantry officer and completed operational tours in Croatia and Kosovo. He has written widely on defence and security issues, receiving awards from the United Kingdom Ministry of Defence, the British Army, the Royal United Services Institute, the US Naval Institute, and the Conference of Defence Associations Institute. He is presently living in London where he is completing a doctoral degree at the London School of Economics. Colonel (retd) Howie Marsh served in several senior military positions in the Canadian Armed Forces as a commander and educator, the Army Inspector, a force developer, and director of army requirements. He has collaborated in the publication of many studies on military leadership, military affairs, and technology. Colonel Marsh lectures on Science and Technology as a strategic determinant and is a senior defence analyst with the Conference of Defence Associations.

The Conference of Defence Associations (CDA) was engaged as a primary partner in this effort. Members of the Conference of Defence Associations Institute (CDAI) in particular were instrumental in assembling experienced people to undertake primary research and others, who contributed information, insights, opinion, and unique expertise to the project. Other members of both organizations read the manuscript, some several times, checking facts and offering advice to the researchers and the editor. Once the manuscript was completed, members of the CDA and CDAI assisted in the presentation of the work to the public and to members of parliament through the CDA's wide network of interested associates.

Too many people were involved in this project to mention them all, but some deserve special thanks for their contribution to the final product. Lieutenant General Richard Evraire (retd), President of the CDA, not only supported the project and the researchers, but also turned his considerable skills as an editor to the manuscript, an effort that is reflected throughout the book. Colonel Alain Pellerin (retd) worked from the beginning of the process as project manager, assembling information and sources, contributing to workshop discussions, and reading and commenting on various research papers. He also brought the work to the attention of "the Ottawa men" in a successful effort to highlight the serious problems here addressed to individuals who might influence future defence policy.

Brigadier General Don McNamara (retd), President of the CDAI, contributed notes and advice and read several of the individual research papers. He brought to the project and to the attention of the researchers and the editor his special insights into the realities of defence policymaking in Ottawa, the "system of systems" that is the Canadian Forces, and the particular situation facing Canada's air force. Dr. Richard Gimblett, "a former naval person," also read the project papers and added his deep understanding of naval strategy and the considerable problems that maritime commanders will encounter as they try to find ways with ever-decreasing resources to turn governments' policy declarations into realities.

Scores of officers and officials are employed in National Defence Headquarters doing essentially what a few researchers attempted to do in this project. These dedicated people understand the seriousness of the defence capabilities problems that will confront the next government. They are, however, mostly proscribed, or at least discouraged, from bringing their personal views into the public light. The researchers owe much to a few of these officers and officials, and we hope that this public project will advance a common national cause.

Military and defence policy problems and the range of solutions that might correct them are not always clearly discernible. Many bright people invariably see complex things differently than others. Some officers and officials truly believe that getting the policy process right and assuming that next year's budget will be larger will solve tomorrow's problems. Others think this rationale is but an administrator's delusion. Nevertheless, it is also fair to say that no one of good sense and experience discounts the seriousness of the consequences for Canadian defence and foreign policy caused by the pending collapse of Canada's military capabilities. It is at this point where insiders and outsiders who may disagree on the details of the problem have no disagreement about the reality of the problem.

This study could not be produced without the continuing service and professional dedication of members and associates of the School of Policy Studies at Queen's University. Particular thanks are due to Lois Jordan, the indispensable assistant to the Chair of the Defence Management Studies program. Moira Jackson skilfully copy-edited the entire work, adding clarity to papers that, at times, too often reflected the habits of authors trained to write for their professional colleagues. The authors wish to thank, as well, Mark Howes and Valerie Jarus for their careful preparation and production of the final text of this edition of *Canada Without Armed Forces?*

Contents

	A National Crisis for the Next Government	xi
1.	The Fundamentals of National Defence Policy Are Not Sound, *Douglas L. Bland*	1
2.	The Capital and the Future Force Crisis, *Brian MacDonald*	25
3.	The Personnel Crisis, *Christopher Ankersen*	55
4.	The Gathering Defence Policy Crisis, *Howie Marsh*	83
5.	A Summary of Major Findings	105
6.	An Alternative Future	111
	Historical Annex	121
	Glossary	129

A National Crisis for the Next Government

> ... we must be prepared to defend our citizens, our economy, our infrastructure, our economic systems, and even our way of life.
>
> *John McCallum*
> *Minister of National Defence*
> *October 2002*

TWO FORCES, ONE PROBLEM

Informed Canadians are aware of the perilous state of the Canadian Armed Forces on active service today. Numerous studies, both public and private, point to the stresses and strains on members of the armed forces and military capabilities resulting from an unprecedented operational tempo and from policies that have demanded for a decade that members of the Canadian Forces "do more with less". It is the crisis of "the present force": a commitment-capabilities dilemma brought on by the gap between the quantity and quality of people, equipment, logistical support, and funding available today and the demands of current defence policies and operations.

What is not as well understood by Canadians and Canada's political community is the national crisis of "the future force". It is a gathering crisis caused by insufficient attention to and funding support for the people, equipment, training establishments, and logistical support facilities, among other things, that are needed to provide credible military capabilities tomorrow. Yet, as serious as this problem is, it is but a symptom of a wider political and policy predicament that will confront the next government of Canada.

The next government will be caught up in a cascading policy entanglement initiated by the rapid collapse of Canadian Forces core assets and core capabilities. This problem will inevitably disarm foreign policy as Canada repeatedly backs away from international commitments because it lacks adequate military forces. In these circumstances, new policy initiatives aimed at "being useful to the United States in our own interests" may well be derailed. When, however, the government moves to solve this capabilities problem, presumably by rebuilding military capabilities, the real crisis will be revealed. The government will find that it cannot achieve this aim before vital Canadian Forces capabilities fail.

Even if the government were to increase expenditure allocations to national defence immediately and substantially, that pending crisis could not be avoided. The time required to replace major equipments, develop coherent military capabilities, and rebuild the "trained effective strength" of the armed forces simply exceeds the mandate of the next government, even if it were to serve a full term. Thus, the true crisis that will be sitting on the doorstep as the next government moves into office will be to find ways to conduct a credible foreign policy and reconstruct relations between Canada and the United States, as the operational capabilities of the Canadian Forces continue to decline through the next five to ten years. At best, the next government might set the Canadian Forces on the road to recovery, but that intent still leaves unfilled the immediate, critical needs of foreign and national defence policies.

This book presents the major findings of a research project aimed at discovering the true nature of the crisis of the future force. The central question for the researchers was this: given past and present policies, what will be the state of core military capabilities in five, ten, and fifteen years? Researchers looked for answers in three main areas of concern: equipment profiles, the Canadian Forces population, and "enabling" or support elements of the armed forces. Studies reveal a *future force* undeserving of this title. Rather – rapidly and then inevitably in five or ten years – Canada's major military equipment will succumb to the combined effects of overuse and technical obsolescence, making them operationally irrelevant. People, described in official Canadian defence literature as "our most valuable asset", with the right balance of age, experience, and training will not be available to replace those who will leave the armed forces over the next several years. Support for equipment and operations is disintegrating, and little can be done to stop it, in some cases because spare parts and technicians are not available and will not be available in the years to come.

Canada is heading for a long period when governments will be without effective military resources, even for domestic defence and territorial surveillance. Even if the next government were to provide nearly unlimited funds in an attempt to overcome this deficit, little can be done before the apprehended crisis becomes fact. The downward slope of the capabilities curve is too steep, and the slide is too fast. Many core capabilities, or essential elements of them, will collapse before operationally effective units can replace them. Canada in a few years will be effectively disarmed.

THE PARAMETERS OF THE RESEARCH PROJECT

Researchers were asked to work within a particular set of ideas and definitions and to concentrate their efforts on the primary subject: the future force. A brief explanation of these research parameters might help readers understand more fully the project and its insights.

The Present Force and the Future Force. Senior military officers and defence officials are routinely concerned with both the present force and its activities and the future force intended to replace it. A coherent defence policy and management system would provide funds for a continuous flow of new concepts, doctrines, equipment, technologies, and people into the present force to maintain relevant capabilities and to transform others as circumstances change. This continuous interaction does not suggest that particular military elements would be mindlessly reproduced year after year. Rather, the "force development process" ought to measure and assess requirements, always looking for "force multipliers" to improve military effectiveness economically and efficiently.

Canada has rarely had such a coherent force-development system in fact. Although eager defence-planners have designed rational management processes for national defence policy, the real process is more commonly random and sporadic. Governments periodically acquire fleets of ships, aircraft, and combat vehicles, and then close off production and future purchases until the next capabilities crisis occurs. In such circumstances, the present force ages and the armed forces works with old equipment until (sometimes) the new process of decision, acquisitions, and operational acceptance comes back to life. Researchers in this project clearly reveal the consequences for this national habit for the Canadian Forces of tomorrow.

The present force and the future force can compete with each other for attention and funding, sometimes so intensely that one becomes the enemy of the other. This unfortunate dynamic is especially evident whenever the Canadian Forces is placed on a fixed budget, which is the usual situation. The present force consumes most of the budget simply to pay salaries and the housekeeping costs of military activities. The capital-investment account gets what might be left over after this overhead has been paid.

Real operations, such as those the Canadian Forces has been conducting since 1990, increase overhead costs, and the only source of funds to pay these bills for a defence policy on a fixed budget is the capital account. Such increases as the government has made to the defence budget in the last few years have been unavoidable contributions to the present force and ongoing operations. But even these additions are not enough to pay for complex operations, as in Afghanistan. Thus, officials are forced, as Defence Minister John McCallum complained, to finance current activities "by raiding the capital budget".[1]

Over the last ten or twelve years, the present force has become the unwitting enemy of the future force, drawing money and attention from projects and programs meant to sustain Canada's core military capabilities. The effect of this dynamic has been so severe and prolonged that the bill to recover the future force is far beyond the means available in existing and predicted defence budgets. The researchers paid very close attention to this dynamic relationship and drew from it a rather disheartening set of conclusions.

A Focus on Capabilities. Researchers were not much concerned with the effects of defence policy on the future of extant military organizations. The primary purposes of defence policy are, after all, to provide military capabilities and put them to proper use. Throughout this report, therefore, researchers avoided framing the data or their conclusions around the institutional interests of the navy, army, or air force. They looked instead at the state of core military capabilities, which are nearly always composed of elements from every branch of the Canadian Forces.

Core capabilities are, in fact, composed of several intertwined elements, mainly trained people, equipment, command and control systems, training establishments, and logistical resources and units. These elements, however, provide little capability if they are simply piled on a jetty. Usable capabilities are created when experienced commanders and trainers meld the elements into operational units. If any one of the requisite elements is missing, or time is not provided for collective operational training, then the supposed capability is defective to some degree. The researchers, individually and together, paid particular attention to the interaction of the parts – the system of systems – noting where they were discordant and/or incoherent.

Thinking from the perspective of capabilities, not of the institution, is important for other reasons. First, the operation of modern armed forces can rarely be divided into service packages. Although the navy, army, or air force may be prominent on certain missions, any recent operation that was completely owned by one service was an anomaly, if only because logistical support in the Canadian Forces is a common function provided by a unified military system. Second, people who suggest that Canada might develop "niche roles" based on one service discount the negative effects such a policy would have on not only foreign policy but also domestic security.

The researchers were convinced that the maintenance of multi-faceted core capabilities would provide governments with the most useful and usable assets to support national security, defence, and foreign policies. The evidence from the missions the Canadian Forces has undertaken over the last ten years supports this conclusion convincingly. Unfortunately, the researchers found little indication that an appropriate range of capabilities can be produced or maintained in the future, mainly because funds are not available to allow for systematic force development, no matter the grandeur of plans on paper. Canada's future force will likely evolve into a small, less coherent mix of parts of core capabilities – something old, something new, and much that is borrowed.

The Military Population. Like many members of the defence community and academia, the researchers had a predisposition that led them to think of "capabilities" as equipment. It followed from this assumption that such factors as the rustout of assets, technological obsolescence, and so on would define the crisis of the future force. It is not a trivial problem, but to the surprise of some, the most serious problem may well arise from the personnel factor.

During the Cold War, the Canadian Forces developed an industrial model for managing people. Citizens were recruited, were assigned to functions, progressed (or not) for 30 years, and retired. Few operational surprises interfered with this pattern, which was established to suit the peculiar conditions of the Cold War – "a war without battles". In the new era, described in Chapter One of this work, the situation is very different. People are being consumed in operations – much as in any past war – and the Cold War model for "human resources management" does not fit these circumstances. Thus, the comfortable profile of the military population is no longer a reliable guide for force planning. Indeed, the researchers found the profile to be seriously skewed, illustrating an imbalance between young people and trained, experienced people. The worrisome fact is that this problem cannot readily be overcome, and trying to do so – by rapid recruitment, for example – seems only to aggravate the situation.

Taking Charge of Remedial Action. Most Canadian governments have provided for their defence policies whatever is available after domestic policies are satisfied. The duty to make something useful from whatever is offered by the government falls to leaders within the defence establishment; members of cabinet hardly ever join in the effort. In the best of times, "just enough" allows officers and officials to cobble together some type of defence program. If planners are lucky, they may find an attentive defence minister who is able to wrestle a bit more from the prime minister. But hoping for such a lucky break is not a sound basis for defence management.

The problems of the future force are now so serious, however, that leaving its management to the usual routine will no longer suffice. The chief of the defence staff and the deputy minister, even with the aid of a sympathetic defence minister, simply do not have the resources or the power to solve the gathering crisis by themselves.

As this research demonstrates, Canada and the government are about to enter a period where there will be few credible resources to ensure Canada's national defence or to pursue an independent foreign policy. This is a matter that requires the urgent attention of the next prime minister, for only he can redirect resources to begin the long recovery of military capabilities, and only he can redirect the governing party and the federal bureaucracy towards this task.

Nor would a responsible political leader want to leave this national priority in the hands of officers and officials – not that they are not competent and trustworthy. Canada's national defence is the responsibility of every Canadian, and politicians through their decisions, actions, and the oversight of the machinery of government must provide direction to this fundamental national policy.

THE 2004 DEFENCE REVIEW

Canada's defence policy will be "reviewed" sometime soon after Jean Chrétien leaves office. Past reviews, as in 1993 for example, have been comprehensive, mainly because of the long periods between them. The next review, however, should not begin on a blank piece of paper. Rich sources of information and opinion on the defence issues and problems of the day can be found in Parliamentary studies, particularly those prepared by the Standing Committee on National Defence and Veterans Affairs (SCONDVA) and by the Senate's Committee on National Security and Defence, in other studies prepared by non-governmental organizations, such as the Conference of Defence Associations, and in internal reports of the Department of National Defence. A careful assessment of these documents, and conversations with their authors, ought to be the first business of any defence review.

The range of options on defence policy open to the next government is more limited, perhaps, than some might suspect. It is unlikely that a review would recommend, for instance, that Canada withdraw from its traditional alliances or, on the other hand, throw itself completely into the grasp of the United States or the United Nations. Some popular commentators suggest that Canada restrict the Canadian Forces to certain "niche roles". This research addresses this idea in detail. But the simple fact is that the Canadian Forces are already niche forces with just enough diverse capability to meet the government's basic responsibilities for defending Canada, cooperating with the United States, and undertaking modest international commitments. These capabilities, as outlined above, are intermingled; that is to say, there are few distinct capabilities that are "sole tasked" to only one objective. Since every core capability contributes to some extent to all of the usual defence objectives, cutting one in favour of some other would only diminish the government's ability and flexibility in meeting necessary domestic and foreign policy goals.

Defence reviews that begin with the assumption that all options are open invariably produce a set of very general recommendations that prove to be of little practical use to defence ministers or senior defence-planners. The next defence review must concentrate on the gathering crisis of the future force and its serious consequences for Canada-United States relations and foreign policy generally. The review, therefore, should have two immediate objectives.

First, the committee ought to provide advice to the government on how Canada is to manage domestic and foreign policy with ever-decreasing military capabilities. The committee might recommend ways in which present force capabilities might be stretched and preserved until replacements come on line.

Second, the committee must construct a future-force programme that would identify high-priority projects and their costs; suggest ways to reform, if necessary, acquisition methods to provide a speedy recovery of failing capabilities; initiate a subsequent full review of Canadian Forces personnel policies aimed at bringing them into line with current realities; and, finally, outline a parliamentary process for overseeing the recovery of armed forces capabilities over the long term.

This type of targeted defence review is without question of the utmost importance, and it is the only sure way to inform the government and the public about the seriousness of the defects in defence policy. The degree to which the prime minister personally directs this review and supervises the recovery of military capabilities will signal to Canadians, the federal bureaucracy, and Canada's allies the extent to which the country is back in the game. A widespread review identified by experts as merely a device for avoiding hard choices or evading the crisis at hand will provide a clear signal that Canada is withdrawing willy-nilly from its national and international responsibilities. If the future force is allowed to fall further into disrepair, then Canada cannot help but become the first modern and major power to disarm itself. The next government's defence policy ought to be directed towards saving Canada from this preventable outcome.

NOTE

[1] McCallum, John, Minister of National Defence, speaking to the Toronto Board of Trade, Toronto, Ontario, 25 October 2002.

CHAPTER ONE

The Fundamentals of National Defence Policy Are Not Sound

Douglas L. Bland

> The key principles of the 1994 Defence White Paper continue to be relevant in today's uncertain international security environment ...
>
> *Canadian Security and Military Preparedness*
> *The Government's Response to the Report of the Standing*
> *Senate Committee on National Security and Defence (2002)*

Ask any senior Canadian defence department official why no public review of defence policy has been attempted nor any new White Paper on national defence policy produced since 1994, and the official will invariably reply, "there is no need of either because the fundamentals set out in the 1994 defence policy paper remain sound." Yet in the summer of 2003, as Canadian Armed Forces units again deployed to Afghanistan on another round of combat duty, it was obvious that "the fundamentals" underpinning today's policy and decisions are not sound.

Almost every 1994 assumption, assessment, and conclusion about the world we live in, the breadth and demands of Canada's explicit and implicit commitments to the international community, the military capabilities Canada needs to meet them, and the funds required to sustain them are seriously weakened or compromised by the facts of international security and defence relations in the world of 2003. Ten-year-old estimates of "how much is enough" for national defence have been proven false. Indeed, the relevance and prudence of every important element of defence policy are open to challenge, if only because too much time has passed since they were last scrutinized critically and comprehensively. The only responsible conclusion one can draw from an assessment of the most critical fundamentals of current policy and the decisions built on them is that they are not sound and that Canada's defence policy as a whole is, therefore, suspect.

Military capability is the essential element among a host of fundamentals that together provide the foundations for decisions on the ends and means of national defence. Reports prepared by the Senate of Canada, the House of Commons, the Auditor General of Canada, various non-governmental organizations – including numerous, credible studies by the Conference of Defence Associations – and others by academics and research institutions all note that the very long-term survival of Canada's military capabilities is in question. Foreign governments and the North Atlantic alliance worry that Canada can no longer carry its share of the defence burden, even in North America. The most telling evidence of all comes from defence establishment studies and military leaders confirming most of these external reports.

This monograph is not intended to rehearse what has already been amply stated in other publications. Rather, its aim is to describe the main findings of detailed research into the future state of Canada's military capabilities. It is clearly evident that if governments continue to manage and fund national defence policy, and the Canadian Forces in particular, within the same policy structure and at near the same activity rate as over the past 13 years, then basic defence capabilities will collapse and the planned transformation of capabilities to meet emerging threats will not be possible. The state of equipment and the lack of capital investment are serious, but the rapid rate at which skilled, experienced leaders are leaving operational units is truly worrisome.

What is even more remarkable is the finding that the rate of erosion of some capabilities is now so steep and accelerating so quickly that even if the government were to act immediately and aggressively to halt the decline, many defence capabilities cannot be recovered before they become militarily ineffective. The rate of decline is too steep and the time required to replace them too long to avoid this end.

Capabilities are composed of several related parts – systems within a system. Merely repairing one part may not solve the gathering crisis because the failure of one element can have a cumulative effect on the whole system and can spread so rapidly as to cripple major capabilities entirely. As one element of a capability comes under stress, then invariably its other components do so as well, causing a deterioration of that capability system. The Canadian Forces medium-range air-transport capability built around the CC-130 Hercules aircraft provides an example of this relationship. Every deployment places greater stress on the aging fleet of Hercules aircraft, raising the demand for spare parts, which are in short supply. Then, for want of spare parts, mechanics cannot do their duty and they leave the service; for want of mechanics, aircraft cannot fly; for want of aircraft, pilots quit; for want of aircraft to fly vital missions, defence policy is endangered. This scenario is being played out across the most important deployable capabilities and military occupations.

Some will point out that the government has recently boosted defence spending, which is true. These new funds, however, are directed mainly at rescuing the present force and ongoing operations of the Canadian Forces: that is, at overhead and the maintenance of existing capabilities even as they, like old soldiers, fade away. The problems addressed in this research are those of the future force, the set of military capabilities that must be prepared today for tomorrow's duties.

Governments have a responsibility for both the present force and the future force. For too long, however, successive governments have made the present force the enemy of the future force by keeping the armed forces on unreasonably low, fixed budgets. Chiefs of the defence staff and officials have been compelled by falling budgets and increasing activity rates in all areas to take funds from the future force – from capital investment – to pay the overhead – the personnel and operations and maintenance bills of the present force. They are, in effect, dumping fuel from the aircraft to lighten its load to get a few more miles before it runs out of petrol and falls from the sky.

The hope, and it is no more than that, is for some event to intercede and save the falling aircraft, some dramatic change to provide a safe haven for the less demanding fundamentals of *1994 Defence White Paper*. But there is no safety in turning the aircraft around nor in circling in place. Canadians must begin quickly and dramatically to reconstitute and transform defence policy, the defence establishment, and the Canadian Forces if they are to confront successfully the evident, not the hoped for, fundamentals of present conditions and the immediate future.

THE FUNDAMENTALLY CHANGED STRATEGIC LANDSCAPE

The ending of the Cold War brought into being "a new world order", a new international relationship among states. But it is not a new order of peaceful international harmony, a situation in which laws, rules, and consensual authority prevail. Since 1989, leading nations have been engaged in political, diplomatic, economic, humanitarian, and military activities to bring such an order to specific regions of the world, as part of a collective effort to establish a wider-ranging order in the international community and to international affairs generally. In the tradition of the invented language of diplomacy and international studies and discourse, this ongoing period of conflict and resolution may be termed the world-order era.

As the Cold War ended, President George Bush, Sr. pronounced the beginning of this "new world order". The phase described more the clear ending of one era without much definition of the new. Order, of course, has several meanings, but President Bush meant at least that the political structure of international affairs had changed. He also implied, purposely or not, that the world had entered some form of peaceful harmony under a new global consensus, if not a constituted authority.

These notions seemed obvious in 1990 with the peaceful conclusion of the Cold War by the superpowers, renewed confidence in the United Nations, and universal condemnation of Iraq and the subsequent United Nations-mandated war against it after its attack on Kuwait. Even as disorder erupted in Yugoslavia, the international community seemed confident in the United Nations and its ability to stop and reverse such disturbances. Faith in the new international order blossomed, not because the United Nations had changed its ways, but because nations now appeared sure that circumstances would allow the United Nations to meet its early promise, at least with respect to controlling lesser states. Moreover, there was little reason to expect conflict among the major powers, dominated as they were by a single superpower, the United States. All these points, among many, were made in *Defence 1994*.

Nevertheless, the new world order of regulated, if not peaceful, harmony depended on several assumptions about how international security affairs would unfold in the future. Chief among these was the hopeful belief that the Security Council could be counted on to judiciously referee disputes between states and to impose its will on lesser states. This assumption stood on the even less stable notion that the permanent members of the Security Council would be able to set aside to some extent their national interests in favour of global interests. The new world order depended on the willingness of the members of the Security Council, with or without the General Assembly's involvement, to use their military, economic, and diplomatic powers to discipline recalcitrant states. Success, however, also depended greatly on the credence that leaders and citizens in uncooperative states gave to pressures applied to them by the major powers.

As the 1990s unfolded, to the surprise and frustration of many politicians and observers, leaders in many parts of the world – in the former Yugoslavia, Somalia, Iraq, Rwanda, and across Africa and the Middle East generally, for example – were willing in pursuit of their own aims to suffer (or rather to allow their citizens to suffer) not only United Nations condemnations, but also significant military force. As communal disasters, regional conflicts, and wars erupted, and no harmonizing authority stood forward to prevent them, the end of the Cold War heralded not so much a new world order as the emergence of a "new world disorder".

Canadians learned once again that harmonious, law-based order is not a natural outcome of international relations. They relearned that if law-based order is the desired goal, then it must be constructed at many levels by the active management of the international system and, at times, by international interventions in the internal affairs of fractious states by the most powerful states. What western defence ministries were learning fast by 1996 was that interventions may require aggressive military operations to remove a state's governing regime, to disarm and arrest lawless factions, or to separate warring bands in civil clashes or in regional conflicts.

Defence 1994 was constructed on the assumption that military activities would decrease in numbers, scope, and scale and, therefore, that capabilities could be reduced, otherwise modified, or even eliminated. On this basis, allocations to national defence could be cut – in some areas, radically. Canadian officials and senior officers, however, began as early as 1993 to understand that military operations, large and small, in this new atmosphere were likely to increase, to be more dangerous, and to attract public attention.[1] Whenever the Canadian Forces were selected as the device for encouraging, imposing, and enforcing order anywhere, whether sponsored by the international community or by states in coalitions of the moment, people noticed. This fact is hardly surprising, even in relatively peaceful encounters, given the directness of military actions, the cost to all parties, and the difficulties experienced in moving from a situation of militarily imposed order to consensual order. Yet warlike, military intervention in international affairs is the cardinal fundamental that is missing from *Defence 1994* and, moreover, the fundamental that officials seemed eager to hide from Canadians as the human costs began to pile up in Somalia, Bosnia, Rwanda, and elsewhere.[2]

Public attention and the costs of these operations were not the only complicating factors for defenders of *1994 Defence White Paper* and the government's policies towards the armed forces and national defence generally in the years after it was announced. Military operations aimed at imposing or supporting with armed force the establishment of order in states or regions have common features. In all but the smallest operations, they usually involve a series of related military operations aimed at achieving a single overall objective. They are, in military terms, campaigns, and it is these "stability campaigns" that became and continue to be the main focus of Canadian defence policy and the military operations that support it. Unfortunately for defence planners and members of the Canadian Forces, the reality, the fundamentals, of these campaigns contradict and clash with the assumed fundamentals of *Defence 1994* and the policy preferences of the Liberal government that is caught up in them today.

Although these campaigns differ in their particulars – in numbers, force type, location and so on – they share several characteristics. The terms and mandates for such campaigns before 11th September tended to reflect an international consensus that supported military operations over long periods, as in the former Yugoslavia, or in other cases, mere "coalitions of the moment", as in East Timor. After 11th September, the new agenda became much more concentrated around the interests of the United States, raising demands on the Canadian Forces at home and abroad. The 1994 assumption of fewer engagements fell by the wayside, and Jean Chrétien became the most hotly engaged, if not committed, wartime prime minister since Mackenzie King.

STABILITY CAMPAIGNS – THE NEW FUNDAMENTAL

Armies and navies and air forces learn on the job, and if defence policy is to be relevant and prudent, it must adjust to the reality of these lessons. Four fundamental differences between the Cold War era and immediate post-Cold War analysis on the one hand, and the new world-order era on the other, are now evident from ten years of campaigning to bring order to, or impose it on, lawless parts of the international system.

- Military capabilities must be radically transformed to meet very different structural, doctrinal, and operational demands created by these world order campaigns.
- Campaigns are now usually conducted in underdeveloped states and regions where conditions impose significant logistical loads of a scope and scale not anticipated in the early post-Cold War era.
- The legacy of Cold War "peacekeeping" and its so-called lessons is dead, and provides no credible guide to defence policy, force development, or military doctrine.
- Finally, the usual schematic for framing Canada's defence missions – the defence of Canada, the defence of North America in cooperation with the United States, and international cooperation in security affairs, as essentially stand-alone missions – is no longer valid because all these activities are now embodied in one unified mission, even when components of that mission are conducted in disparate regions around the globe.

Military Capabilities. The term "military capability" means much more than a mere collection of equipment. It is defined as a composite of technologies, equipment, trained people, command structures, doctrines, and logistical support; that is, a system of systems planned and able to work efficiently together. Modern (meaning, in 2003) armed forces, essentially those of NATO member states, have evolved since the end of the Cold War into smaller, professional, highly technical, and more lethal multipurpose forces. They possess, singularly in the case of the United States and in some combined allied formations, capabilities to continuously assess military situations, to detect opposing forces and attack them from safe havens, to deploy and manoeuvre large formations rapidly around the world, and to sustain them in difficult environments indefinitely. Taken together, these capabilities define overwhelming military power.

Yet, with the exceptions of the Gulf War and operations in Iraq in 2003, the stability campaigns have been conducted mainly by small units and formations using modern versions of traditional weapons and tactics. Certainly, these campaigns and associated operations benefit enormously from capabilities developed to fight wars during the Cold War era. Nevertheless, the application of military means in the world-order era is fundamentally different, arguably the antithesis of the means that essentially characterized the entire Cold War era. As the Cold War era was defined by nuclear weapons, so the world-order era is defined by the modern infantry soldier. It is the infantry, as it was in other periods of military history outside the Cold War anomaly, that provides the indispensable requirement of the stability campaigns, "a foot on the ground". In naval stability operations, where blockade, sea control, and the interception and "inspection" of commercial vessels in the littoral are common, the defining weapon is as much the versatile frigate as it is the aircraft carrier battle group. The naval campaigns of the 1990s suggest a strategic-era notion reminiscent of the days when "sea control" maintained maritime order and supported mercantile (and colonial) objectives, and "gunboat diplomacy" controlled wayward states and regimes.

The normative purpose of every campaign in this new world-order era has been, and will be in the future, to establish an orderly, reasonably safe environment to allow and enable political and civil authorities to work with the local population towards building a harmonious society of "peace, order and good government." Dominance is the key military concept in these stability campaigns. Military operations, therefore, are premised on two cardinal assumptions: first, that the purpose of the armed force is to impose and maintain order on the local populations by all necessary means; and second, that violent confrontations are to be expected and defeated during the entire operational period. Where intervening armed forces are themselves the personification of "good order and discipline" and are adequately equipped and trained for the types of duties known from experience to be necessary in such campaigns, then an enforced order will usually prevail.

Areas of Operation. Although proxy wars and diplomatic and intelligence operations were carried on worldwide, the Cold War was essentially bounded by Europe (broadly considered) and North America. The world-order era, on the other hand, is global in breadth, defined in NATO terms during the last ten years as "out of area". Such regions, especially in Africa and the Far East, present significant complications for the usual contributing nations, including the United States. Stability campaigns have been conducted near the edge of most nations' deployment capabilities. The transportation of forces, and their sustainment in Africa and some other regions, is a complicated matter of great expense, made more so by the fact that only the United States has adequate long-range military transportation systems. As a result, force options tend to be limited to small, "light" formations. Often such units are adequate for the task at hand, but this limitation does restrict missions and may impose on the deployed force a high degree of risk that might not be necessary if transportation systems were more capable and the operating environment less forbidding.

Distance is not the only or the most limiting factor in such campaigns. In many areas, even in the Balkans in some respects, the climate and the terrain pose significant operational problems for troops and commanders. Ironically, the environment can degrade the technical capabilities of equipment that supposedly gives modern forces their advantage over native forces in these campaigns. Significant costs are imposed on the deployment and sustainment of forces and their safety during operations by crude transportation networks, inferior or nonexistent technical infrastructure, primitive communications systems, miserable economies, dangerous, endemic diseases, and the lack of potable water, local sources of food, and shelter for high-tech military communications and for medical units. These factors, among many, tend to limit the number of states that can contribute to missions and to increase the resources that more capable states must provide to less capable coalition armed forces to ensure their effective participation in stability campaigns.

"The ground" is a constant factor and a variable in military planning, not only at the local level but also at the strategic level. Where one plans to fight and the environment in all its aspects there often dictate how one will fight. Whole schools have evolved around desert, jungle, and urban warfare, leading to doctrines, tactics, force structures, and equipment for these special circumstances. Decisions and planning are complicated by other layers of detail, such as whether operations will be troubled by irregular tactics, hostile populations, neighbouring states, and biological threats. Taken together, considerations about where and in what circumstances operations will be conducted have a significant influence not only on current campaigns but also on fundamental national decisions about defence policy, strategy, doctrine, and force structure over the longer term.

It is in these areas that the experiences of the stability campaigns of the 1990s are most evident. Of all the underlying factors, few are as important as the assumption that the campaigns of the future will be fought in faraway places of which our leaders, commanders, and troops know very little and where technical advantages drawn from the Cold War may not provide the return hoped for in other, more familiar places.

France, for example, has a large, sophisticated, nuclear-capable armed force. But its 2003 deployment into the Democratic Republic of Congo to secure a small region in that state was deemed by French officers as "highly risky", underscoring the asymmetry between military capabilities developed for the Cold War and those needed for the world-order era. France's problems also highlight the great difficulty for modern states of bringing the full force of their military capabilities to bear even on weak states and violent organizations in these circumstances.

Nations are slowly – and in some case, reluctantly – adjusting their military force structures and range of capabilities as stability campaigns in distant underdeveloped lands become the operating norm for their armed forces. Defence-procurement programmes are shifting from heavy mechanized formations to lighter, more easily transportable formations. More money is being directed towards air- and sea-lift capabilities and to rapidly deployable logistical units. The ability to put firepower on targets remains a key criterion for weapons systems, but technology and the demands of experience gained on past stability campaigns are moving programs towards lighter, smaller, more accurate weapons that can be handled by fewer soldiers. Navies have adopted or are developing doctrines for "littoral warfare" in support of ground operations and other tactics, not only to project power from the sea but to maintain control of the seas. Only the United States has the means and the will to hold ready a full range of military might on the scale required for global warfare. Other states are making more limited choices, and those choices are conditioned by the assumption that their armed forces will most often be called to join stability campaigns in support of international order.

The End of Peacekeeping. Stability campaigns and operations are not peacekeeping as the term and concept were understood throughout the Cold War era. Although the ends of peacekeeping and stability operations may be similar – the establishment of a harmonious order leading to permanent peace – the operating principles of the two are significantly different. Stability campaigns are not policy-free; that is to say, forces are deployed in most instances to achieve goals openly related to the interests of the contributing nations, even though at times their policy motives may be shaded by egalitarian rhetoric.[3]

Neither the civil authority nor their force commanders assume that stability campaigns will be "impartial" affairs, as is the case in United Nations-mandated peacekeeping operations. In every campaign and operation mounted since 1989, the convening authority has identified a party or parties, if not as belligerents, then as the group or groups to be controlled. This conceptualization has significant implications for the way military forces conduct operations, when units decide it is necessary to use force, and how they use it. Military commanders leading stability campaigns do not consider themselves or their subordinates as referees between contending parties engaged in a dispute. Rather, they tend to operate on the assumption that their soldiers' duty is to impose, reinforce, and maintain order – by force of arms, if necessary – in the pursuit of peace, order, and good government, as the mandating organization or state specifies. If in doing so they must apply force disproportionately against one faction, then that is a decision that will be made after an assessment of the circumstances that commanders confront. But military leaders are no longer as inhibited as traditional peacekeepers usually were by the notion that if they must apply force at all, then they must do so evenly, regardless of the situation.

Certainly, members of armed forces in either situation must act in accordance with the laws of armed conflict. But whereas in peacekeeping scenarios the use of force is exceptional (arguably even in Chapter VII missions), in stability campaigns both the intervening force and the subject community understand (or should) that force will be used at the discretion of the commanders, not only to defend their units but also offensively to advance the mission they are assigned and to impose order on the contending groups.

True believers, some scholars, and others bent on particular interests have tried to rescue traditional peacekeeping by attempting to modify its methods while holding to its ideological roots. They speak, for instance, of "muscular peacekeeping"[4] and use other terms intended to place stability operations in a collective security harness. Such arguments, however, soon become entangled in a web of conflicting concepts incompatible with the realities of the world-order era.

The most egregious example of this confusion occurred in the early days of "peace operations" in the former Yugoslavia, where soldiers were commanded to act within traditional peacekeeping ideas while they were caught in the midst of a small war. A Canadian solider who was seriously wounded in this action recognized his situation clearly: "This is not peacekeeping; this is war-monitoring."[5] But neither peacekeeping nor war-monitoring is suited to circumstances where the establishment of order through the appropriate application of force is the only sensible response to people who are intent on "winning" by bloody conflict and are undeterred by the outraged and unarmed protests or by the supposed moral authority of the United Nations and the imagined global community.

The Symmetrical Canadian Defence Mission. Another fundamental difference between the assumptions of *Defence 1994* and the new world-order reality touches on the very essence of traditional Canadian defence policy. From at least 1945, defence policy was based on territorial divides. According to Cold War thinking, Canada's defence required forces deployed to meet three objectives: the defence of Canada, the defence of North America in cooperation with the United States, and international choices, which generally meant missions originating in NATO and in the United Nations. Forces, doctrines, command arrangements, capabilities, and all aspects of defence management were designed around this framework, and they produced missions, armed services, capabilities, and "requirements" that were distinctly different from each other. *Defence 1994* faithfully followed this traditional formula, with predictably disjointed results as the international demands on the armed forces changed radically from post-Cold War precepts to the realities of the world-order era.

After 11th September and the beginning of the anti-terrorist campaign directed by the United States, the traditional formula became even less relevant to Canada's national defence and international relations. It may now be harmful if it remains the basis of the conceptual framework for defence policy. Today, there can be no difference or distinction in policy or force structure in these areas. The defence of Canada is inseparable from the defence of North America and from the imposition of order in other specific regions of the world. The destruction of terrorist bases in Afghanistan and naval interdiction in the Arabian Sea are examples of the extension of the campaign to defend Canada at home by acting abroad. This symmetry of missions and commitments is a cardinal characteristic of the new era and, if acknowledged, will have a profound effect on national defence planning.

Finally, and of great importance for those planning for Canada's future armed force, is the fundamental fact that continuous warfare – a conceptual innovation in itself – defines the strategic circumstances of the international system. Although wars and conflicts may be settled in one region and a sort of peace brought to another, the general and immediate causes of these types of disturbances will continue across the globe far beyond the foreseeable future. Continuous warfare may be defined as wars that endure in various degrees and intensity without end, simply because no belligerent has the power to overcome any other. Characteristically, these wars involve military and paramilitary forces, "low-tech" weapons and devices, intermingled military and political authorities, contrasting and contradictory aims, intense fighting interspersed with "cease fires", and truces followed by the resumption of disorder. Often "total war" in limited theatres is the rule, and scant consideration is given to non-combatants, traditional icons, or cherished institutions. Indeed, these very things may be the preferred targets on all sides.

This style of warfare, different in most important respects from usual notions of "total warfare", "limited warfare", and "irregular warfare" (classically fought in support of a regular army), has become the preferred method in civil disputes and for weak states in conflicts with each other and even with powerful enemies. It is also the obvious defence for regimes under attack by forces of order, including forces deployed by major powers or under the full authority of the United Nations. Given that most states are weak and conflicted to some degree, then we should prudently anticipate that the next ten years will be a repeat of the last ten years of continuous warfare in desperate places around the world. Even in areas in which order of a sort has been imposed, the norm may be disorder, even state suicide. Sadly for the intervenor, there is, by definition, no exit strategy from continuous warfare.

These new fundamentals have greatly influenced the reality of Canadian Forces operations and Canadian foreign-policy decisions since 1989. They have also, willy-nilly, driven defence-policy decisions, large and small, and in the circumstances changed the direction of declared policy in fact. The attention of officers and officials in National Defence Headquarters has shifted from the administrative routine of the early 1990s and the habit of "lending troops", to other more immediate concerns, not just for the deployment of forces but for their command and employment according to Canadian laws and standards.

However these outcomes may benefit today's Canadian Forces and defence policy generally, they consume the precious time senior officers have for thinking about future national defence to the detriment of critical force-development issues. Many officers and officials do spend their days looking forwards, but they are handicapped into impotence by the lack of money to develop the forces they see as necessary to Canada's national defence in the future.

The most basic new fundamental is completely opposite to that presented in 1994. Rather than a world of falling commitments allowing for fewer, less costly capabilities, the Canadian Forces today faces a world only faintly perceived in 1994. Canada lives in a world of more commitments conducted in circumstances that are enormously costly in people, equipment, and political attention. Some political leaders might have supposed in 1994 that their post-Cold War vision would allow the Canadian Forces to gradually drift into irrelevance. Unfortunately, for them and many others, that vision is now but a dream departed. Nevertheless, the consequences of holding onto that dream – so evident in the government's reluctance to change its fundamental policy assumptions – may be seriously disrupting the future possibilities for Canadian foreign policy and national defence.

THE NEW FUNDAMENTALS OF CANADA-UNITED STATES DEFENCE RELATIONS

Some Canadian officials might not think that the fundamentals of Canada-United States defence relations have changed since 1994, but Americans (insofar as they pay attention to the issue) certainly do. The changes are evident, for instance, in America's dramatically altered national-defence strategy, in its defence and security organization and international commitments, and in the administration's attitudes towards "old Europe", and they break the easy rhetoric and assumptions that underpin Canada's defence policy today. The most significant change, however, is the change in American citizens' perception of their security at home and their growing alienation from so-called traditional allies. It is a state of mind reflected vigorously in the policies and actions of President George W. Bush.

The unremarkable sentences in *1994 Defence White Paper* outlining Canada-United States defence relations simply repeat the unreflective wisdom of the Cold War relationship. The relationship, we are told, is "close, complex, and extensive." No matter what Canada might do to protect itself, "Canada would still be obliged to reply on the US for help in protecting its territory and approaches." Implicit in this pronouncement is the self-assuring belief that the United States would always be obliged to protect Canada in its own interest. It is faith based on the Cold War assumptions about the value of Canadian territory to the United States – a faith strongly held, even in 2003, but blind to the strategic and political significance of the rapid transformations in American military technology that are overtaking this fundamental of Canadian defence policy. This transformation and its political consequences for Canadian policies are hardening into fact, as the National Missile Defence project demonstrates, and recovery for Canada may now be beyond our reach.

Safety for North America after the fall of the Soviet Union was, according to Canada's 1994 defence policy, premised on the continuing reduction of intercontinental ballistic missiles and reductions of nuclear and other chemical and biological weapons. The government in 1994 was cheered, moreover, by the stability of the international disarmament regime and especially "American ... adherence to the strict interpretation of the 1972 *Anti-Ballistic Missile Treaty*" and its policies that future missile defence systems that would be "consistent with existing [1994] arms control agreements." Canada, according to *Defence 1994* "retains an influential voice in US defence policy formulation" and "access to significant defence-related information" from the United States government, defence agencies, and armed forces.

One is hard-pressed today to accept as sound any of these fundamentals, even if they were meant to apply in only the strictest and narrowest

North American interpretation of Canada-United States defence relations. But, of course, that was never the aim for this section of *Defence 1994*, which obviously described but one element of a wider, indeed, global, allied defence relationship. But that global relationship, too, has been altered beyond recognition, especially so after the government's pointed refusal to consider supporting President Bush's strategy to deal with the tyrannical regime in Iraq.

Nice arguments could be made about the precise timing of the failure of easy assumptions of Canada's defence policy towards the United States. There have been stark moments, none more so than the attacks of 11 September 2001. But even without this horrid day, American defence strategy shifted perceptively once George W. Bush replaced President Clinton in the White House. Under Clinton, America stood on the defensive and allowed threats against the nation's interests and citizens to grow almost without challenge. The attacks on New York and Washington may have occurred on President Bush's watch, but they were assembled under Bill Clinton's unwatchful eye.

At the moment the political guard changed in Washington, if not before, any Canadian government alert to the fundamental importance of Canada-United States defence relations would have begun (at least in private) an extensive review of all issues touching on Canada-United States foreign and defence policies. This review was more urgently required once President Bush confirmed his administration's campaign promises and quickly made the most far-reaching and radical changes in United States defence and foreign polices since 1947.

These promised new directions were presented plainly and unequivocally in *The National Security Strategy of the United States of America* in September 2002.[6] But so far as research into public records and other primary sources reveal, no Canadian review of the implications of this strategy on Canada's defence situation has been conducted in Ottawa. Certainly, the realities of what some Americans now call "the Fourth World War" have not caused Canadian ministers to spring to the garrison's walls. Rather, the fundamentals of defence policy meant for other times stand stubbornly unaltered, even late in 2003. Canada-United States defence relations as set out in *Defence 1994* are fatally flawed and beyond redemption – without question, these fundamentals of defence policy are not sound.

THE NEW FUNDAMENTALS OF DEFENCE MANAGEMENT

The radical change in international security and defence affairs, when combined with niggardly defence spending from 1989 to the present, inevitably affected the management of defence policy throughout the period. Not only are the strategic fundamentals of policy no longer sound, but the fundamentals of defence administration in Canada have been shattered as well.

While combat capabilities were being dismantled at the end of the Cold War, bureaus for managing the surviving force grew. National Defence Headquarters (NDHQ), designed in 1972 to meet Cold War commitments and the demands of the Ottawa officialdom, remained essentially unchanged in structure throughout the 1990s. Concepts for managing most parts of the defence program also stayed static, largely unresponsive to the actual needs and circumstances of the new reality.

Cold War-era defence management in Canada was built on the assumption that each year would follow the next in a never-ending stable pattern. Management systems for personnel, procurement and acquisition, supply, and budgeting were, by and large, fashioned around this steady state and the assumption that war was highly unlikely. The argument could be made, especially after 1970, that the management of defence trumped the operations of defence. Moreover, the priorities of defence planners for decades lay in the future force, often at the expense of the present force.

In the post-Cold War era, the main aims were to hold to proven policies, husband scarce resources, and restrict the effect of operations on the day-to-day business of national defence. Gradually, however, the costs and circumstances of the world-order era wore into the system, creating serious contradictions between operational realities and bureaucratic preferences. Nevertheless, the tail tried hard to keep its control over the dog. The concepts underlying three central managerial functions no longer seem adequate to the situation and circumstances of national defence in 2003. The fundamentals of defence management are not sound.

Personnel. The general assumption behind Cold War and post-Cold War personnel policy was that service in the armed forces was a career. It followed as a fundamental of 1994 defence policy that this highly trained, long-service force would be unchanged and available to effect defence policy. Personnel policies, therefore, continued under the Cold War, industrial, "cradle to grave" career model suitable for an armed force where people were expected to serve the colours from recruit to sergeant-major, from officer cadet to chief of the defence staff. Operational duties were, of course, included within the model, but mostly only as a routine part of "career development."

War and operations in the 1990s interfered with but did not change this scheme. People were killed and wounded in the field, many suffered mental injuries, and young members of the Canadian Forces began to leave the armed forces worn out from constant assignments overseas. Indeed, every fundamental notion about recruitment, training, service, benefits, and post-service care developed for the Cold War era failed to fit the realities facing the Canadian Forces in the 1990s and afterwards. People serving in the core land, sea, and air combat and support trades – the people most needed to fulfil the actual wartime policies of the government – soon began to leave the Canadian Forces early, and they continue to do so. As experienced leaders depart, few are left to train replacements and thus both quantity and quality are eroding together. By 2003, continued deployments and operational stress had changed the composition of the Canadian Forces and the assumptions of post-Cold War policy. Clearly, the fundamentals of personnel policy must change also.

Logistics, Equipment Acquisition, and Life-Cycle Management. During the Cold War, Canadian defence planners depended on a well-developed national and allied scheme to provide logistical support to deployed forces. Among other things, agreements and "host nation support" relieved somewhat the burden of national logistics planning, and NATO "interoperability" allowed national forces to share supplies, such as ammunitions and fuels, with each other. The theatres of operation were mostly determined, and to some degree stockpiles were established to meet at least initial operational requirements. Furthermore, the Canadian Forces planned to conduct operations in highly developed societies possessing sophisticated infrastructures.

These agreements and civilian establishments, moreover, set the requirements for Canadian and allied military transportation capabilities, which were created to operate over short to middle distances and from modern facilities. Even peacekeeping missions were rather easily managed because they were small and logistical demands were routine. Logistical plans and requirements were, therefore, relatively uncomplicated and reasonably assured. But no matter the wartime plan, the dominant fundamental of the Cold War and post-Cold War logistical system was the assumption that there would be no war, but if war came, then there would be plenty of time to move from the extant peacetime system to the planned (but rarely tested and unreliable) wartime system.

After 1991 and the first deployments into the former Yugoslavia, things began to change abruptly. As mission piled on mission, the Canadian Forces' logistics and supply system was increasingly strained to cope with the realities of these missions. Although it tried mightily to make the reality fit policy's fundamental assumptions, the system was found wanting in every category, despite the great efforts of members of the Canadian Forces to make do. The underlying problem was the realization in NDHQ that adjusting to the operational missions would be expensive and cause considerable disruption to the established policy, procedures, and interests. The hope and expectation were that the "crisis" in the Balkans or in Somalia or wherever would pass, allowing a return to "proper soldiering". Each decision to wait for a return to "the fundamentals" of Cold War and post-Cold War policy aggravated logistical problems in the field and delayed any review and reform of basic logistical concepts. As the Canadian Forces deploy into Afghanistan once again, it is plain that the fundamentals of operational logistics are not sound.

The management of equipment in the Canadian Forces since before 1994 has been based on a "life-cycle system". In other words, major classes of equipment are acquired on the assumption that they will be in service for a predictable period. These assets are then managed, or their use rationed, to meet this life-cycle timetable; every other aspect of the equipment's life and support needs – for spare parts, for example – is calculated within this framework. The system works reasonably well so long as the activity rates, flying hours, mileage allowances, and so on can be carefully controlled, as they could be during the Cold War and would have been under the hopeful assumptions of the *1994 Defence White Paper.*

The realities of the war operations of the 1990s and those continuing today have overturned this fundamental assumption of defence policy. Not only are all the major assets of the armed forces being used at rates greater than planned, they are being subjected to harsher treatment because of the nature of their employment and the regions in which they are employed. "Life-cycles" are shorter, spare parts are being consumed at higher rates, and vehicle casualties are increasing the demands on technicians and repair facilities. Thus, for a combination of reasons, fewer pieces of essential equipment are available to support defence policy. Before 1994, these problems might have been managed by simply restricting activities and user rates, but this management fundamental of the Cold War period has largely been overtaken by the realities of the new world-order era, in which activities will not conform to logisticians' plans and demands.

During the Cold War era, defence planners and other government officials assumed that they would have plenty of time during the life cycle of any major equipment to acquire its replacement or substitution. Although there were many who complained about the long time needed to acquire equipment, most everyone accepted the system as it stood. Besides, there was hardly ever any real need to speed up the process because there was no emergency, nor was one likely.

This fundamental of defence policy continued into the 1990s (and not only because of policies within DND). But this policy assumption, like the life-cycle management system, is no longer sound, because it does not fit the realities of the new era. As operational use increases, life cycles are cropped. Equipment-acquisition cycles, therefore, must be shortened accordingly. This requirement increases demands for capital expenditures as higher usage rates of extant equipment increase the costs of Operations and Maintenance (O&M) across the Canadian Forces. Moreover, the obsolescence of current equipment has been accelerated by the demands of operational commanders and promises by government that "the troops shall have what they require", and by the rapid rate of military technical innovation. Thus, a key fundamental of 1994 defence policy – that budgets can be reduced because activities can be controlled and reduced, thus prolonging equipment life-cycles – is obviously invalid.

Defence Budgeting. For a very long time, governments have allocated to their national defence policies whatever funds they had available, not what reasonable people thought was needed. During most of the Cold War after 1956, politicians assumed that they could safely follow this custom because war was not imminent and commitments and activities could be cut to fit defence-policy cloth. Indeed, those who launched the Canadian Forces into Somalia in 1992 allegedly followed this formula, shaping the force to fit budgetary requirements but not operational requirements. A fundamental assumption emphasized during the crafting of *Defence 1994* was that customary ways of managing defence spending would suffice in the 1990s and beyond; in fact, the government demanded nothing less.

The customary way hangs on a certain inevitable dynamic. The defence budget is most easily understood when it is seen as three baskets of goods or costs: people; O&M, or services and housekeeping; and capital expenditures. The defence minister, the chief of the defence staff (CDS), and officials live within a fixed income and, in a type of zero-sum game, must balance one basket of goods against the others. The competition, however, is rarely fair, and discretion is greatly restricted. The first allocation must go to people and the second to pay for O&M, the two making up the defence-policy overhead or, in other words, the commitment to the present force. Whatever remains may be allocated to the capital account, and it is this residual that provides the only flexibility or discretion within the budget. When, however, overhead increases, then capital decreases and fewer resources are available to build the future force. This is the situation, as this book will illustrate, that has confronted defence planners throughout the 1989-2003 period.

Again, the fundamental assumption in 1994 was that commitments and budgets could be reduced. The reality in the 1990s and the early years of the new millennium, and in the foreseeable future, however, is also that commitments in difficult circumstances that consume people and resources at wartime rates cannot be avoided if Canada's preferred foreign policy is to be sustained. When budgets are held to what is available and increases are made only to service the defence-policy overhead, then capital and the future force suffer.

During the Cold War, the customary budget dynamic was managed for better or worse by planners who had a high degree of control over costs. They could, for instance, reduce activity rates – training, for example – and thus reduce O&M costs. Personnel strengths could be lowered to provide money for capital acquisitions and so on. These exercises effectively ended after 1994 for two reasons: the government insisted that the Canadian Forces be maintained at 60,000 personnel, and planners lost almost complete control over activity rates because they were war-related, not mere peacetime, exercises. The only flexibility remaining was in the capital account, and it was raided, year after year. Raiding the capital account may be a useful short-term expedient from time to time, so long as the loss in one period can be recouped in another. Throughout the past ten years, however, the fall in the capital portion of the budget has been relentless, and the damage is cumulative.

Planners of experience assume today, as they did in 1994, that about 23 percent of the annual defence budget must be allocated to the capital account to maintain essential capabilities. The account has never reached this level and, therefore, carries an accumulated deficit equal to the sum of foregone allocations of past years. In other words, if the 23 percent figure is a reasonable target for capital spending (and no minister disputes it), then for many years adequate funds have not been available to rebuild military capabilities, and the decline becomes steeper each year as defence budgets fail to hit the 23 percent target for the capital account. But that target was established under the assumptions of declining use of the armed forces. It cannot, therefore, be a reliable figure in 2003 because the deficit in the capital account is too great and the depreciation of capabilities is too steep (from unplanned usage and rapid obsolescence) to be overcome by a figure meant for less demanding circumstances.

Some might complain that this dynamic is merely an accountant's game, but as this book will show, the negative effects of under-investment in capital, in the future force, have in fact placed defence policy in a worrisome situation. The figures and the effects are there in official documents for all to read. The 1994 fundamentals of national defence stood on the assumption that there would be sufficient funds – if not in 1994, then eventually – to hold major capabilities in such a state that the Canadian Forces would be "able to fight the best alongside the best." The fundamental policy after 1994 as expressed in documents such as *Strategy 2020* was that the Canadian Forces could be transformed into a light and agile force built on the precepts of the so-called "Revolution in Military Affairs" and able to fight "interoperably" alongside the armed forces of the United States. These fundamental notions cannot be sustained with the resources available in 2004.

A RECOVERY?

Missing the approaching change in international affairs in the early 1990s is no fault. Most "experts" bought into the new world-order scheme, and politicians everywhere in the West leapt at the idea because it seemed to offer security without cost. The fault in Canada lies in not responding to the changes in the fundamentals of national defence once the need was evident, which arguably occurred in about 1995. The greater fault, and it rests in the hands of a few political leaders, lies in continuing blindly onwards without pause while driving the Canadian Forces more deeply into harm's way and using people and resources with reckless disregard for future needs.

If the fundamentals had been dispassionately reassessed in 1995-96, then Canada might have begun to reconstitute its defence capabilities sooner, probably as soon as the federal fiscal deficit had been mastered. Had this course been followed, then the present and gathering crisis in defence and foreign policy might have been avoided. Leaders cannot plead that they were unaware of the need to change the fundamentals of defence policy in the face of the barrage of information, public and private, that was put before them, especially after 11th September. Yet they let the matter slide.

Now, in 2003, the crisis caused by willful disarmament is upon the nation and threatens the country's hard-won and honourable place in the international community of like-minded nations. Canada's sovereignty, seemingly placed absentmindedly in the hands of others through neglect of the instruments of national security, is increasingly unsure. The fidelity of Canada's political community to the nation's traditional liberal-democratic allies and to the interests and values Canadians have defended with them in peace and war is an open question in capitals worldwide.

Yet, as these pages will attest, there is not much Canadians can do to save this situation, at least not in the term of the next government or even the next government after that, perhaps. The descending slope is too steep and it will take too long to turn it upwards for tomorrow's government to benefit from altered policies. Managing this dangerous period between falling and recovering military capabilities is the essence of the gathering crisis. Nevertheless, leaders today can begin the process of reconstituting Canada's armed forces and, by doing so, lead Canada back to its rightful and responsible place among the free, liberal democracies of the world.

NOTES

[1] Canada, "PCO Meeting – Peacekeeping Operations." Memorandum from ADM Policy Kenneth Calder to Deputy Minister Robert Fowler and CDS General John De Chastelain (Ottawa: Department of National Defence, 30 March 1993).

[2] For evidence, see the award-winning documentary, *A Question of Honour*, Volume 2 (Toronto: Stornaway Productions, 2002).

[3] Critics might declare that "traditional peacekeeping" was always concerned with national or allied interests, and that is certainly fair comment. True-believers and most of the United Nations bureaucracy over time would dispute this argument, saying that peacekeeping operations and negotiations associated with them were primarily aimed at non-state purposes. Critics of the United Nations might respond that, insofar as this was the case, it explains only why, in their view, the United Nations and its deployed forces can and have often become "part of the problem."

[4] See Alex Morrison *et al., Peacekeeping with Muscle: The Use of Force in International Conflict Resolution* (Cornwallis Park: The Lester B. Pearson International Peacekeeping Centre, 1997).

[5] *A Question of Honour*, Volume 1.

[6] United States, *The National Security of the United States of America* (Washington, DC: The White House, September 2002).

CHAPTER TWO

The Capital and the Future Force Crisis

Brian MacDonald

> For an extra $130 Bucks ...
> *Senate Standing Committee on National Security and Defence*
> *November 2002*

THE STRATEGIC CAPITAL GAP

From the moment a new military equipment platform enters service, it is immediately subjected to two forces of depreciation. One is the wear and tear that comes through use over time – the physical rustout factor, which can be handled through proper maintenance until the equipment reaches the end of its service life. The other is the much faster process of technological rustout, a process that itself is driven by the rate of technological change in the civilian field of Information and Communications Technology (which drives the potential for change in the capabilities of military technology) and the rate of military-capital investment in new capabilities (a process that is now primarily driven by the United States, the global leader in military technology innovation).

In earlier times, it was possible to handle both physical and technological rustout by means of planned "Mid-Life Refits" of major platforms. These refits dealt with the physical deterioration that was beyond the capacity of routine maintenance and, at the same time, allowed for the replacement or upgrading of the platform's technological systems to the current standard.

The two Gulf Wars demonstrated the importance of technological modernization. The side with the technological advantage gained an important combat advantage on the battlefield. For example, a key element in the "Revolution in Military Affairs" is the parallel "Revolution in Target Acquisition". First Target Acquisition (FTA) provides a significant advantage in determining who survives in one-on-one combat between armoured vehicles, in combat aircraft, or in artillery/target engagements. The criticality of FTA is driven, in turn, by the "Revolution in Weapons Accuracy and Lethality," which guarantees a 95 percent probability of a first-round hit if the target has been accurately located. Moreover, contemporary weapons effectiveness now virtually guarantees a kill when the target is hit. Put another way, the single-shot-kill probability of leading-edge weapons is now approaching 1, as the US M1A1 Abrams main battle tanks so clearly demonstrated in the Second Gulf War.

Since advances in military technology are now so driven by developments in civilian Information and Communications Technology (ICT), there is now a growing recognition of the increasing impact of the rapidly shortening life cycle of civilian technology and of the increasing disconnect between it and the much longer physical life-cycle of the military platforms on which that technology is mounted (and especially between it and the length of the increasingly problematic cycle of military procurement). With an ICT manufacturing cycle of two years and a usable civilian ICT life cycle of five years, militaries the world over face the need to spend increasing proportions of their capital-renewal budgets on technology upgrades of existing platforms. When platform replacement becomes necessary, the *required* capital share of defence budgets increases sharply, whereas in the post-Cold War world the *actual* capital share fell sharply (a phenomenon particularly acute in Canada).

Another consequence of insufficient capital budget allocations is the need to extend the planned lifetime of major equipment. The rapidly increasing costs of maintaining rapidly aging equipment, in turn, increases the strain on the maintenance dollar and further limits the amount of capital-renewal money available. For Canadian policy-makers, what is becoming increasingly apparent as one of the major consequences of the erosion of the capabilities and availability of major platforms and of the accompanying decline in readiness rates is the decreasing influence of the Canadian military in Canadian foreign and security policy.

The "strategic capital gap" (the gap between capital needs and capital funds) is today an even more significant problem than it was when the late Professor Rod Byers, first Director of the York University Research Programme in International and Strategic Studies, coined the famous "Commitment/Capability Gap" phrase at the end of the decade of the 1970s – a period that former Conservative Party Defence Minister Perrin Beatty later so aptly termed "The Rustout Decade" of the Canadian Forces.

A critical task for Canadian defence planners and analysts, then, is the identification of:

- the critical physical and technological life-end points of major capability platform fleets;
- an estimate of the costs of their replacement and of the capital funds available for their replacement; and
- an estimate of the future capital-investment needs for "transformation".

This chapter addresses these issues.

THE EFFECTS OF PHYSICAL AND TECHNOLOGICAL AGING ON PLATFORM LIFE-CYCLE PLANNING

The Effects of Aging on O&M Costs

Increased age brings with it the requirement for steadily increasing repair and maintenance costs, which themselves may limit the amount of money available for platform renewal.

The Congressional Budget Office (CBO) of the United State Congress, in a report to the Senate Budget Committee, noted that "O&M dollars that are spent directly on operating and maintaining military equipment – to pay for fuel, purchase or repair parts, and overhaul weapon systems at depots – account for a relatively modest share (about 20 percent) of total O&M expenditures today."[1]

Nearly half of that 20 percent, approximately 9 percent, is devoted to the "purchase of repair parts", defined as "actual expenditures on consumables, such as washers, filters, and gaskets", and "depot-level reparables" (DLRs), such as spare parts, avionics, and engine components. Those costs, combined with fuel costs, are what are often referred to as "steaming-hour", "flying-hour", or "tank-mile" costs. Fuel accounts for 4 percent of O&M costs, and the remaining 7 percent is spent on "Major Overhaul at Depots", which "includes spending on the inspection, maintenance, and repair of military equipment, excluding DLRs, at large public (Department of Defence) and private (contractor) depots."

While the Report acknowledges data problems in the various studies it reviewed, it concluded that "CBO's analysis of the relationship between equipment costs and age, which focused on Air Force and Navy aircraft ... indicates that aircraft do become more costly to maintain as they age. CBO estimates that spending on O&M for aircraft increases by 1 percent to 3 percent for every additional year of age, after adjusting for inflation."

Dr. Raymond Pyles of the RAND Corporation, in testimony before the United States House Committee on Armed Services, provided a similar analysis, noting that as aging aircraft went through periodic heavy-maintenance sessions, the cost of each session rose sharply.[2] He pointed out that the cost, in constant dollars, of the seventh heavy-maintenance session (called for in the case of a 40-year-old aircraft) would be between five and nine times more expensive than the cost of its first heavy-maintenance session, normally carried out some five years after delivery. He noted that a similar pattern would be expected for commercial aircraft.

The CBO Report also addressed the question of "downtime", reporting that its review of prior studies revealed that "Equipment's age can affect readiness as well as maintenance costs.... Analyses of the time between breakdowns and the time spent fixing equipment also indicate that age has an effect. According to those studies, an additional year of age may decrease the time between breakdowns from 1 percent to 7 percent and increase downtime from 1 percent to 9 percent."

One particularly telling case study cited by the CBO Report pertained to the KC-135 Tanker aircraft, a variant based on the now elderly Boeing 707.

> The KC-135 Stratotankers, many of which are 40 years old, are some of the oldest aircraft the services operate. And they are becoming more expensive to operate; the cost per flying hour increased from $8,539 in 1996 to $11,128 in 2000 (after adjustments for inflation).[3] The military has little or no experience operating and maintaining aircraft of that age, and no commercial airline fleets of a comparable age exist. Consequently, the [U.S.] Air Force recently began collecting data to enable it to predict how long or effectively those aircraft can continue to operate.

As the KC-135 tankers age, they require more maintenance, reducing the number of aircraft available for operations. For example, between fiscal years 1991 and 1995, the labor hours planned to complete depot overhauls of the KC-135s increased by about 36 percent, and the average time aircraft spent in the depot increased from 158 days to 245 days. According to Air Force officials, the growth in planned work included time to apply compounds that prevent corrosion and to rewire significant portions of each aircraft. In addition, according to a report by the General Accounting Office, "Shortages of spare parts, that were no longer in production or stocked, and unplanned work, required to correct structural corrosion and fatigue, contributed to maintenance delays and reduced aircraft availability."

As the following two cases indicate, the Canadian experience bears out the American one.

The CC-130 Hercules Case Study
Journalist Chris Wattie quoted a Canadian Air Force briefing document that stated:[4]

> Almost two-thirds of Canada's fleet of CC-130 Hercules transport aircraft, the workhorse of the Canadian air force, is currently listed as "unavailable," the *National Post* has learned, grounded by growing maintenance problems, a shortage of trained mechanics and old age.

According to the air force, he reported, the biggest factor influencing the availability of the Hercules is wear and tear: "Canada's fleet of CC-130 Hercules transport aircraft logged 17,934.6 hours [of flight time] in 2002-2003 ... Given that nearly 60 percent of the fleet is from 35 to 39 years old, it should come as no surprise that Canada operates the highest-time military CC-130s in the world."

Wattie noted that the shortage of airworthy Hercules is also due to a maintenance system that is becoming overloaded by the responsibility of keeping the aging aircraft flying: "The resources available to handle CC-130 maintenance ... have become increasingly inadequate and hard-pressed." As well, a shortage of spare parts and longer waits for periodic maintenance checks – extensive inspections and preventive repairs conducted every few months – have kept many Hercules on the ground. Experienced aircraft technicians are in short supply after a recruiting moratorium of almost 10 years, imposed during the mid-1990s by federal budget cuts. According to Wattie, the document reports, "The combination of an ageing aircraft fleet, parts shortages, declining technician qualification and experience levels is resulting in increased inspection times and declining aircraft serviceability."

His story was followed by a Canadian Forces Press Release,[5] dated 24 July 2003, which reported that the Air Force is being forced to reduce by 30 percent the planned flying hours of the Hercules fleet in 2003/4. 1 Canadian Air Division Commander, Major-General Marc Dumais, himself a former Hercules pilot, was quoted as saying: "A high operational tempo and an aging fleet have combined to reduce the number of available aircraft to the point where it became obvious that 16,200 hours was the most appropriate YFR [yearly flying rate]. We are projecting a slight increase to 17,100 hours next year."

The Press Release went on to report:

> The 19 older E-model Hercules in use by the Canadian Air Force are the highest-time military Hercules in the world, with most having accumulated between 40,000 and 44,000 flying hours. As the aircraft age, the time required to complete periodic inspections, which are conducted every 900 flying hours, has increased. As well, the Progressive Structural Inspections, conducted by a contracted maintenance facility every 3,600 flying hours in concert with a periodic inspection, also consume more time.

The troubling thing about this issue is that the fundamental problems of the Hercules fleet have been known for some time and are, in fact, worse than this overview indicates. In 2001, the Auditor-General of Canada noted that in 1990/91 the CC-130 fleet was flying about 35,000 hours per year, but that rate had declined by about 37 percent by 1999-2000.[6] The further reductions announced in 2003 will represent a decline of 54 percent from the 1990/91 levels, bringing the annual flying hours down to only 46 percent of the 1990/91 total, for a fleet that is absolutely critical to our ability to mount or support international operations or to provide assistance to the civil authority at home.

The Auditor-General also found "significant increases in the ratio of total maintenance hours to flying hours from 1990-91 to 1999-2000, namely, 62 percent for the Hercules. In the Hercules fleet, corrective maintenance accounted for most of the increase. Even though the Hercules flew about

37 percent less in 1999-2000 than in 1990-91, total hours of corrective maintenance increased about 26 percent; the ratio of corrective maintenance hours to flying hours doubled."

The Sea King Case Study
Then there is the perpetual saga of the Sea King helicopters.

The Chief of the Defence Staff, General Ray Henault, noted in a June 2003 Round-Table with media[7] that "... as we know the equipment, the mission equipment, in ... [the Sea King] is now obsolete ..." The CDS further noted that "maintenance of an aircraft of that nature, like the Sea King, starts to demand more time and obviously more energy and more money to maintain".

Brigadier-General Colin Curleigh, former Commander of Maritime Air Group, referring to *the Sea King* Weapon System Support Plan (WSSP) 1998-2003, dated 4 September 1997, provides an insight into the technological depreciation problems of old airframes:[8]

> The first objective is the vital one which deals with effective management to ensure the *Sea Kings*' "airworthiness is preserved for the duration of the current ELE [Estimated Life Expectancy – which is now to the end of the year 2000] and in anticipation of an ELE extension to 2005 or even 2010." Its main provisions include the major structural repair of the centre section, re-routing and clamping of fuel lines, strengthening the tail wheel support assembly, and adjusting the centre-of-gravity by moving mission equipment.
>
> The second objective, supportability, deals with matters that could improve the cost-effectiveness of maintenance and repair and includes such items as major modifications to the engines and main gearboxes of the whole *Sea King* fleet. These modifications were driven by the fact that our *Sea Kings* are the last users of these critical drive-train components, and spare parts are becoming costly and difficult to obtain. Additionally, the transmissions are starting to produce problems leading to increasingly expensive inspection and repair at the contractor.
>
> The third objective is Improved Capability, and as expected, is approached with extreme reluctance for the old *Sea Kings*. It includes replacing the ancient mechanical navigation system (a reminder of the old WWII ARL

tables) with used hand-me-down systems from the USN. With the success of the prototype of the Forward Looking Infrared (FLIR) detector in recent Peacekeeping and SAR Ops, it has been decided to install FLIR mounts and wiring in all *Sea Kings*, and play musical chairs with the 10-12 FLIR sets in the DND inventory. Some components of the unreliable and overloaded electrical power supply system will be improved. Trials are continuing on a Self Defence System that can be quickly installed if the need arises, such as during the Gulf War. The system will include such components as a Radar Warning Receiver, Missile Approach Warning, and Counter Measure Dispensing equipment.

The Auditor-General commented in 2001 that "the Sea King fleet's availability declined from about 42 percent to 29 percent; departmental officials estimated that about half of that decrease was due to downtime for several aircraft modifications and other avionics upgrades, and the rest was for repairs to keep the fleet airworthy." Then there is the "Abort Rate Problem", which represents "the total number of suspected failures per 1,000 flying hours that result in cancellation of a mission." The figures provided by the Auditor-General indicated that the "Abort Rate" for the Sea Kings rose between 1990/91 to 1999/00 by about 50 percent, from approximately 42 per 1,000 flying hours to about 61 per 1,000 flying hours.[9]

The current extent of the cost to maintain an aircraft already 40 years old, with "obsolete" mission equipment, was revealed by a May 2003 Sun Media article, later amplified in *Defence Policy Review*.[10] It was reported that DND had just signed a contract with IMP Group of Halifax, NS, to handle depot-level maintenance of the Sea Kings for a minimum of five years. It also included six additional one-year options, which could extend the service life of this platform (with "obsolete mission equipment," according to the CDS) to more than 50 years, at a potential total cost of $148–307 million.

The Effects of Aging on Operations

The operational impact of the problems of "beyond life expectancy" operation of an aircraft such as the Sea King is predictable. The Auditor General's 2001 Report said:

We reviewed 61 post-deployment reports on the use of the Sea King aboard ships from 1 April 1995 to 31 March 2000. We found that 54 of the reports mention at least one of the following problems: scheduled mission that was cancelled for aircraft maintenance; mission degraded by aircraft's lack of serviceability; poor serviceability that had a negative impact on training; major snags that caused significant downtime; and aircraft that were grounded.

The worrisome comments in the post-deployment reports on Sea King serviceability problems, cited by the Auditor-General, included the following:[11]

High unserviceability
"I can honestly say that in the 17 years I have spent in the Sea King community, through all my deployments, this is the first time I was sincerely embarrassed to be associated with this helicopter, due to her constant and consistent unserviceability and resultant air detachment inability to contribute meaningfully to the ship combat capability or the force in general." (NATO deployment, 10 August to 15 December 1998).

Poor serviceability had a negative impact on training
"As can be seen by Salty Dip 1/95 [an exercise nickname], more than one Sea King may be required to successfully complete the exercise. In this case, five aircraft were used in only three and a half flying days. This meant that subsequent aircraft were not completely equipped and valuable training was missed." (Salty Dip exercise, 11 to 20 April 1995)

Availability of aircraft lowered motivation and morale
"The limited operational capability and availability of the CH-124A had a profound impact on the motivation and morale of the members of the detachment. Many found it difficult to rationalize the motivation required to work extremely long hours to make airworthy an aircraft that was rarely fully mission-capable and, even when mission-capable, of extremely limited tactical benefit to the ship." (Work-ups, HMCS *Iroquois,* 31 May to 26 June 1999)

THE RUSTOUT CRISIS OF MAJOR CF PLATFORM LIFE-EXPECTANCIES

Tables 2.1–2.3 provide a quick means of understanding the rustout dilemma of the Canadian Forces. They include the numbers in each major platform fleet, the year of the initial delivery of the fleet, and estimates of the expected service life of each fleet. Except where otherwise noted in the tables, they are based on figures provided by the Congressional Budget Office of the United States Congress to members of the Senate and House of Representatives.[12]

The shaded portions of the tables provide a quick visual indication of the age of the platform in comparison to its expected service life. Light grey cells indicate ages of less than 50 percent of the expected service life; dark grey indicates an age between 50 and 100 percent of the expected service life; black indicates age in excess of 100 percent of the expected service life.

These tables do not, however, show the age of the platform in relationship to its technological service life. This is now a more critical issue than physical service life, since the technological life-cycle is so much shorter than the physical life-cycle of military platforms. In earlier times, mid-life refits took place at the half-life point of platform life-expectancy, at about 10 years. Nowadays, technology mid-life refits should probably be done at shorter intervals, particularly as platforms are increasingly being given physical life-extensions well beyond their original expected service lives, as cost-reduction expediencies.

H. Lee Buchanan, U.S. Assistant Secretary of The Navy, Research, Development and Acquisition, commenting on service-life-extension programmes (SLEPs) for US aircraft carriers, states that "the life extension program will often cost as much as half the initial purchase price of the carrier. What you get back is another 50 percent extension on its life."[13]

However, life extensions beyond original expected physical service lives are becoming increasingly controversial because there is a clear pattern of rising annual maintenance costs for each additional year of service life, and there may be increases in the operational unavailability of these life-extended platforms, as well.

From these tables, it can be seen that in the five-year short-run period (from 2003-2008), an immediate crisis appears in five critical areas: maritime (medium-transport and ASW) helicopters, the two Auxiliary

Table 2.1
Canadian Navy Major Platform Life-Expectancies

Platform	Number	Date of Origin	Service Life (CBO)	Age 2003	Age 2008	Age 2013	Age 2018	Age 2023
AOR/ALSC	2	1969	35	34	39	44	49	54
CADRE	4	1972	35	31	36	41	46	51
Submarines	4	1989/3	33	14	19	24	29	34
Frigates	12	1992	35	11	16	21	26	31
MCDVs	12	1995	30	8	13	18	23	28

Table 2.2
Canadian Army Major Platform Life-Expectancies

Platform	Number	Date of Origin	Service Life (CBO)	Age 2003	Age 2008	Age 2013	Age 2018	Age 2023
M-109s	76	1971	20-30	32	37	42	47	52
MLVW	2769	1982	20[14]	21	26	31	36	41
MBTs	114	1978	30	25	30	35	40	45
HLVW	1212	1992	20[15]	11	16	21	26	31
LSVW	2879	1993	20	10	15	20	25	30
M113A3	289	1965/2003	15-23[16]	1	6	11	16	21
AVGP	401/301	1976/2004	15-23	0	4	9	14	19
BISON	199	1990/2004	15-23	0	4	9	14	19
COYOTE	203	1996	20-30	7	12	17	22	27
ADATS		1996	20-30	7	12	17	22	27
LAV III	651	1998	20-30	5	10	15	20	25

Table 2.3
Canadian Air Force Major Platform Life-Expectancies

Platform	Number	Date of Origin	Service Life (CBO)	Age 2003	Age 2008	Age 2013	Age 2018	Age 2023
Mar Hel	29	1963	30-35[17]	40	45	50	55	60
CC-130E	19	1963	30-40	40	45	50	55	60
CC-130H	13	1975	30-40	28	33	38	43	48
CF-18	80	1982	20-30	21	26	31	36	41
LRPA	16	1980	30-40	23	28	33	38	43
Tac Hels	78	1994	20-35	9	14	19	24	29
A310	5	1987	40?	16	21	26	31	36

Oiler Replenishment Vessels (AORs), the Medium Logistics truck fleet, the earlier set of 19 CC-130 medium airlifters, and the Army's M-109 Self-Propelled medium howitzers.

The Canadian Forces are already at the edge of the extinction of their sea, land, and air operational-transport capabilities.

Estimating the Cost of Replacing New Platforms/Capabilities

In attempting to estimate the costs of replacing platforms (recapitalizing capabilities), an undertaking that the previous tables suggest could be carried out in a series of five-year periods, this analysis will make the simplifying assumption that the delays inherent in the Canadian procurement process can be removed as a limiting factor.

It might be useful to point out also that considerable difficulty exists in estimating total programme costs for purchases of major equipment, given that total cost typically includes such additional items as an initial set of spare parts, simulators and other training devices, initial training of maintenance personnel, and the costs associated with regional-benefit considerations in letting government contracts (a practice found in most industrialized nations).

The DND Director General of Public Affairs (DGPA) recently hosted a Round Table[18] for defence analysts, concerning the Maritime Helicopter Replacement Project. In the discussion, DND officials revealed that the total current planned cost for the programme was $3.1 billion for 28 helicopters: $1.9 billion for the flyaway costs of the helicopters, plus $1.2 billion for the non-aircraft portion, which would cover such items as those mentioned above (figures expressed in Canadian dollars throughout, unless otherwise specified). In other words, the non-aircraft cost increment was planned to be about an additional 63 percent on top of the initial flyaway cost.

As well, for offshore purchases, figures must be adjusted for differences in exchange rates. When the $US exchange rates rise and fall against the Canadian dollar, the cost of imported American equipment rises and falls accordingly. These changes can be – and usually are – very costly. Table 2.4 provides some indication of the possible programme costs of purchasing certain American platforms to replace aging Canadian ones that have hit, or are about to hit, the end of their life cycles.

Table 2.4
Possible Programme Costs of US Platforms if Selected for Canadian Use

Replacement Platform	Number to Replace	Country of Origin Cost (US$ millions)	Exchange Rate 5 July 2003	Programme Cost (63%) Increment	Final Cost per Platform (C$ millions)	Programme Total Cost Estimate (C$ billions)
CC-130J	19	$87[19]	1.3368	1.63	$189	$3.6
FMTV[20]	2769	200[21]	1.3368	1.63	438	1.2
Joint Strike Fighter	80	54[22]	1.3368	1.63	117.7	9.4
F/A-18E/F	80	71.5[23]	1.3368	1.63	155.8	12.5

Canadian cost figures cited in Table 2.5 were obtained from a variety of sources: existing DND estimates published in various *Long Term Capital Expectations Plans (Equipment)* or *Strategic Capabilities Investment Plans* documents; Industry Canada documents on Shipbuilding, and Industrial Marine figures on possible federal procurement of Shipbuilding and Ship Repair services; and finally, current figures on items listed in the Department of National Defence Reports on Plans and Priorities Status of Major Capital Equipment Projects.

Table 2.5
Canadian Estimates of Replacement Platform Programme Costs

Platform to Be Replaced	*Number to Be Replaced*	*LTCP (E) 2002 Total Cost Estimate ($ billions)*
Maritime Helicopters	28	3.1(2003 update)
CADRE	4	5.3
MLVW	2,769	0.838
Strategic Lift Air/Sea[24]		3.5
ALSC		2.3
AVRP[25]		0.2
New Capabilities		
Land Forces ISTAR[26]		0.63
Joint: CFISR		0.975
Joint: Polar Star		0.685
Joint: Nat Mil Sp Capability		0.270
Life Extension/Modernization		
Frigate LIFEX[27]		2.0
Aurora LIFEX		0.72
SELEX[28]		0.4

ESTIMATING AVAILABLE CAPITAL FUNDING: BREAKING OUT THE CAPITAL BUDGET

A detailed review of the Canadian Defence Budget – particularly the allocation of the budget between capital procurement, personnel, and operations and maintenance – shows the extent to which the hands of the Canadian defence-planners are tied.

The difficulty becomes even clearer when the size of the defence budget is examined, over time, as a percentage of the overall Canadian economy, since it provides a view of the impacts of both inflation and economic growth on the actual "purchasing power" of the defence dollar. Just before the end of the Cold War, in 1985-1987, the Canadian defence budget accounted for 2.2 percent of Canadian GDP. In 2001-2002, the Canadian defence budget accounted for only 1.1 percent of GDP – a decline of 50 percent.

This drop in the defence budget was parallelled by cuts in the size of DND, as regular personnel strength went from 89,000 in 1989 to 60,000 – a cut of 33 percent. Similar cuts were made in the civilian-employee strength of the department, and bases and facilities determined to be surplus to requirement were closed.

A problem facing defence-planners is the fact that the real purchasing power of the defence budget fell 50 percent faster, and farther, than did the cuts to the size of the department (33 percent). The effects of such a difference in shrinkage rates had a particularly significant impact on the capital budget – the part of the budget that can be cut most easily – simply by not issuing new contracts for the purchase of capital goods.

Table 2.6[29] provides a historical perspective of this process by showing the percentages of the defence budget devoted to major sub-categories during the post-unification period. The divisions are those used in reporting Canadian defence budget expenditures to NATO. In a purely Canadian analysis, the "Equipment" and "Infrastructure" columns are often combined into a single "Capital" figure.

What is striking about the post-Cold War period is the sharp drop in both the equipment and personnel shares of the defence budget, and the equally sharp increases in the infrastructure and operations and maintenance shares of the budget.

Table 2.6
Historical Canadian Defence Budget Sub-Divisions (Percent)

Period	Personnel	O&M	Infra-structure	Equipment	Eqpt. + Infras.
Avg 70/74	65.6	24	2.4	7.3	9.7
Avg 75/79	60.8	27.3	2.0	9.0	11.0
Avg 80/84	50.7	29	1.6	17.8	19.4
Avg 85/89	46.2	31.5	1.7	19.7	21.4
Avg 90/94	49.7	29.1	3.2	18.1	21.3
Avg 95/99	44.3	38.4	4.1	13.2	17.3
Avg 00/02	43.4	39.8	4.5	12.2	16.7

In the Rustout Decade of the 1970s, the decision to retain a personnel establishment too large for the available budget led to massive erosion in equipment procurement. In the current rustout decade, the infrastructure and operations and maintenance budget lines are crowding out both the personnel and equipment shares of the defence budget.

However, these figures must be divided between, on the one hand, those sums spent on construction, equipment for permanent infrastructure (such as the increasing numbers of "Simulators" used for training, and various other equipment items attached permanently to buildings rather than to operational platforms in the field environments), and major-equipment mid-life refit and life-extension projects, and, on the other hand, those sums spent on the actual acquisition of new equipment to replace those platforms that no amount of further life-extension spending can possibly hope to sustain.

DND's *Report on Plans and Priorities 2003-2004*[30] provides this further breakout, shown in Table 2.7, which is broadly consistent with the NATO figures:

Table 2.7
Current Sub-Divisions of the Canadian Defence Capital Budget 2003/04

Category	% of Capital Budget	% of Defence Budget
New Platforms/Capabilities	44.4	7.0
Refits/Life Extensions	27.9	4.4
Total Equipment	*72.3*	*11.4*
Infrastructure Construction	11.1	1.8
Infrastructure Equipment	16.6	2.6
Total Infrastructure	*27.7*	*4.4*
Total	**100**	**15.8**

Unfortunately, the four-year forecast from the *Report on Plans and Priorities 2003-2004* provides little hope of significant change in the immediate future. Table 2.8, taken from the *Report*, provides a short-term four-year forecast.

Table 2.8
Current (2003/04) Departmental Canadian Defence Budget Forecast

Year	Total ($ billions)	Growth (%)	Capital ($ billions)	Growth (%)	Capital Component of Budget (%)
2002/03	12.89		1.94		15.05
2003/04	13.51	4.8	2.05	5.7	15.17
2004/05	13.62	0.8	2.12	3.4	15.56
2005/06	13.75	1.0	2.24	5.7	16.3
Mean	**13.44**		**2.09**		**15.52**

The *total* capital component of the defence budget is now in the 15–16 percent range. The equipment portion, however, based on the NATO figures, has fallen to about 11.5 percent: a 50 percent shortfall from the oft-announced, but never achieved, policy objective of spending 23 percent of the defence budget on capital procurement.

MODELLING CF MAJOR PLATFORM RECAPITALIZATION

For modelling purposes, then, it is useful to begin with two simplifying assumptions: first, that the overall defence budget will remain flat in 2003/04 constant-dollar terms, and second, that the available proportions of the defence budget devoted to the four categories cited will also remain constant at 2003/04 levels. These assumptions provide one-year and five-year total capital-expenditure figures as follows:

Table 2.9
Modelling the Canadian Defence Capital Budget Forecast ($ billions)

Period	New Platforms	Re-fits/Life Extensions	Infrastructure Capital	Construction Capital	Total
1 year	0.92	0.583	0.347	0.232	2.09
5 years	4.6	2.92	1.74	1.16	10.45
To 2020 (18 yrs)	16.7	10.5	6.25	4.18	37.6

The next step is to perform a sequential analysis of defence budget capital demand, availability, and shortfall by five-year periods. This can be done by identifying those platforms that will reach the end of their expected service lives during each period, those requiring mid-life refits or life extensions, and required new capabilities. An estimate of the costs in 2003/04 dollars of replacing them can be developed, as well as an estimate of the total capital available. The shortfall is then easily calculated.

For simplicity's sake, the infrastructure capital and construction capital can be treated as constants during the periods, except for the first period, for which the infrastructure equipment bill is known from the *Report on Plans and Priorities*.

The Immediate Five-Year Plan: 2003-2008

Table 2.10a shows the projected costs of new capabilities, old platforms expiring within this five-year period and their estimated replacement costs (cited in the *2002 Long Term Capital Expectations Plan (Equipment)*, except where noted), and aging platforms requiring life-extension refits.

Table 2.10a
Projected Costs for New Capabilities, Major Platform Replacement, and Refit/Life Extensions 2003-08

New Capabilities				*Total Cost ($ billions)*
Joint: CFISR				1.0
Joint: Polar Star				0.7
Joint: Nat Mil Sp Capability				0.3
Land Forces: ISTAR				0.6[31]
			Sub-Total	***2.6***
Replace Platform	*Number*	*Replacement*	*Cost Per Unit ($ millions)*	*Total Cost*
CC-130E	19	CC-130J	200[32]	3.8
MLVW	2769	FMTV[33]	0.438	1.213
M-109	76	None	4.8[34]	0.365
Maritime Hel	28	?		3.1
MBT	114	Stryker AGS?	4.8[35]	0.547
Destroyers		?		5.3
AORs	2	?		1.8
			Sub-Total	***16.13***
New and Replacement Equipment			**Total**	**18.73**
Refit/Life Extend				
Frigates	12		100	1.2
Aurora LRPA	16			0.7
			Total	**1.9**

Table 2.10b shows the available capital funds and shortfall, using the FY2003/04 model forecast.

Table 2.10b
The Bottom Line 2003-08 ($ billions)

Category	Funding Available	Cumulative Prior Years'[36] Commitments	Real Availability	Demand	Shortfall/ Overage
New and Platform Replacement	4.6	-0.5	4.1	-18.725	-14.625
Modernization/ Life Extension	2.92	-0.9	2.02	-1.9	0.12
Infrastructure Equipment	1.74	-0.2	1.54	-2.0	-0.46
Infrastructure Construction	1.16	?	1.16	1.16 ?	$?
Total	**10.42**	**1.6**	**8.82**	**23.785**	**-14.965**

With a total capital demand of $23.8 billion, a real capital-funding availability of $8.0 billion, and a recapitalization shortfall of $15 billion, it is clear that the capital-equipment crisis will arrive in the 2003-2008 time-frame. The shortfall in the capital account is $3 billion per year over the next five years.

The effect on CF operational capabilities will be the complete loss of logistics sea-lift, air-lift, and land-lift capabilities. With only 13 of the newer CC-130s (vintage 1970s) and five Airbuses surviving, the task of undertaking and supporting any but small, uncomplicated international or domestic operations, even within Canada, will be problematic. The loss of the AORs and destroyers makes any deployment of a Canadian naval task group outside Canadian waters nearly impossible without major assistance from allies or contractors, which has obvious implications for independent foreign or defence policies.

Thus, the ability to meet the commitments made in *1994 Defence White Paper* – to be able to deploy army and naval forces to "participate in multilateral operations anywhere in the world under UN auspices, or in the defence of a NATO member state"[37] – will disappear within the immediate (2003-2008) time-frame. It may be possible to avoid the destroyer problem by means of a second refit/life-extension, but the example of the DELEX programme, which extended the life of the previous steam-driven destroyers until the frigates arrived, is not an encouraging one. These types of "fixes", moreover, add to already burdensome O&M and personnel costs.

The Second Five-Year Plan: 2008-2013

Table 2.11a shows new capabilities, old platforms expiring within this five-year period and their estimated replacement costs (cited in the *2002 Long Term Capital Expectations Plan (Equipment)* table, except where noted), and aging platforms requiring life-extension refits.

Table 2.11a
Projected Costs for New Capabilities, Major Platform Replacement, and Refit/Life Extensions 2003-08

New Capabilities				*Total Cost ($ billions)*
Estimate: 50% of previous period				1.3
			Sub-Total	*1.3*
Replace Platform	*Number*	*Replacement*	*Cost Per Unit ($ millions)*	*Total Cost*
HLVW	1212	HLVW adj	0.400[38]	0.484
LSVW	2879	LSVW	0.135[39]	0.389
			Sub-Total	*0.873*
New and Replacement Equipment			**Total**	**2.173**
Refit/Life Extend				
A310[40]	5		20	0.1
Tac Hels[41]	100		4.3	0.43
Submarines[42]	5		80	0.4
			Total	**0.928**

Using the forecast based on the FY2003/04 model, the available five-year capital is shown in Table 2.11b.

Table 2.11b
The Bottom Line 2008-13 ($ billions)

Category	Funding Available	Cumulative Prior Years' Commitments*	Real Availability	Demand	Shortfall/ Overage
New and Platform Replacement	4.6	-14.625[43]	-10.025	-2.173	-12.198
Modernization/ Life Extension	2.92	0.1	3.02	-0.928	2.092
Infrastructure Equipment	1.74	-0.46	1.28	-1.2 ?	0.08
Infrastructure Construction	1.16	?	1.16 ?	-1.16 ?	0?
Total	10.42	-14.985 ?	-4.565	-5.461	-10.026

*"Cumulative Prior Years' Commitments" cells contain the total capital-renewal shortfall/surplus from the first five-year period.

The good news is that only two major platform fleets expire in this period, and only three platforms hit the mid-life refit/life-extension point. The bad news is that capital availability is not sufficient to recover from the capital shortfall of the previous period. With the funds available and predicted, the government could, perhaps, deal with either the shortfall for the deployable, land-based capability or for the sea-based capability, but not both – in effect, making the decision to have either a land-based or a sea-based operational capability, but not both. The really bad news is that there is absolutely no capability for preparing for the approaching and massive demand for capital renewal over the five-year period.

The Third Five-Year Plan: 2013-2018

Table 2.12a shows new capabilities, old platforms expiring within this five-year period and their estimated replacement costs (cited in the *2002 Long Term Capital Expectations Plan (Equipment)* table, except where noted), and aging platforms requiring life-extension refits.

Table 2.12a
Projected Costs for New Capabilities, Major Platform Replacement, and Refit/Life Extensions 2003-08

New Capabilities				*Total Cost ($ billions)*
Estimate: 50% of previous period				1.3
			Sub-Total	***1.3***
Replace Platform	*Number*	*Replacement*	*Cost Per Unit ($ millions)*	*Total Cost*
M113A3	289	LAV	3.4[44]	1.0
CC-130H	13	CC-130J	200[45]	2.6
LRPA	16	MMA[46]	200 ?	3.2
CF-18	80	JSF/FA-18E[47]	118-171	9.4-12.5
			Sub-Total	16.2-19.3 ?
New and Replacement Equipment			**Total**	17.5-20.6 ?
Refit/Life Extend				
Coyote/LAV III[48]	755 est			0.050
ADATS[49]	26			0.343
MCDV[50]	12			0.246
			Total	0.594

Using the forecast based on the FY2003/04 model, the available five-year capital is shown in Table 2.12b.

Table 2.12b
The Bottom Line 2013-18 ($ billions)

Category	Funding Available	Cumulative Prior Years' Commitments*	Real Availability	Demand	Shortfall/ Overage
New and Platform Replacement	4.6	-12.198	-7.598	-17.5/20.6 ?	-25.098/28.198 ?
Modernization/ Life Extension	2.92	2.092	5.012	-0.594	4.418
Infrastructure Equipment	1.74	0.08	1.82	-1.2 ?	0.62
Infrastructure Construction	1.16	?	1.16	-1.16 ?	?
Total	10.42	-10.026	0.394	-20.454/23.554	-20.062/23.16

*"Cumulative Prior Years' Commitments" cells contain the total capital-renewal shortfall/ surplus from the two previous five-year periods.

Like the 2003-08 period, this is a period of a massive re-capitalization requirement that is fraught with difficult assumptions on the aircraft side, where the bulk of the requirement for capital renewal lies. Chief among them are the actual form and cost of the Multi-Mission Maritime Aircraft (MMA) and whether the Joint Strike Fighter, which is supposed to be a reduced-cost platform, will achieve those economies. The F/A-18 D/E cost is included only to give a sense of the possible upper boundary of the cost.

Whereas the primary question of the previous period was whether Canada would choose to have a deployable, land-based capability or a sea-based capability, the primary question of this period is which of the three services will survive, for the capital available clearly shows that funding will provide for only one – or perhaps 1.5 services at best.

SOME VERY UNPALATABLE CONCLUSIONS

The cynical conclusion is that *1994 Defence White Paper* commitments "to participate effectively in the defence of North America, NATO-Europe allies, and victims of aggression elsewhere" are mere rhetoric. The requirement for capital renewal to meet these goals is vastly in excess of the amount of capital monies available to the DND over the next fifteen years. The reality is that either the government's commitments of *1994 Defence White Paper* must be greatly modified, or the capital component of the defence budget must be increased by $2-3 billion per annum beginning in 2004/05. In any case, there is little possibility in the next few years that the Canadian Forces could met these objectives simultaneously – as the worldwide campaign for order now demands – even if the government adopted immediately a program of defence renewal.

Failing that infusion of necessary capital, and without a clear policy direction, defence planners will be driven to continue to use a series of expensive ad hoc and stop-gap strategies to cope with increasing operational demands amidst falling capabilities.

One such strategy might be to delay decision points on capital renewal in the hope that some future government will finally provide enough capital to replace the current status quo. This strategy would be based upon the concept of a strategic life-extension programme for major platforms. It is a sensible short-term survival strategy, provided that one understands that it is based upon the assumption that a reinvestment of 50 percent of the original capital cost of the platform in a Service Life Extension Program (SLEP) will provide a 50 percent increase in the physical life of the platform, which is not always the case.

Unfortunately, such a strategy suffers when the *technological life-cycle* of a system is very significantly shorter than the *physical life-cycle* of the system, such that the physical life-extension is not matched by an identical technological life-extension. This contradiction would have two unwelcome financial consequences that would exacerbate the ongoing crisis in capital-equipment renewal. First, the capital costs needed for additional technology refits over the extended life of an aging platform would increase the diversion of funds from other demands. Second, maintenance costs inherent in holding onto old platforms would escalate exponentially, indirectly taking even more funds from other projects.

Moreover, operational readiness would fall because of the increasing downtime for refits and maintenance, which would gut the real operational capabilities of the Canadian Forces. The Sea King saga is a classic example of the long-term costs of the SLEP strategy, as was the DELEX programme in a previous period.

There is some evidence that this process has already started. A comparison of the Long Term Capital Expectations Plan (Equipment) in *Defence Plan On-Line 2002/03* (extensively referenced in this document) with its successor in *Defence Plan On-Line 2003/04*[51] shows that the CADRE project in the 2002/03 Plan for the replacement of the four Tribal Class Destroyers, which contain the Area Air Defence and Command and Control capabilities for a Canadian Naval Task Group, has disappeared. There is now talk of a second SLEP for the elderly Tribals, which would extend their life to 2020, when they will be 50 years old. There will be, of course, a reluctance to pour any more money into technological renewal than is absolutely necessary for a ten-year life extension, leading to a repeat of the Sea King experience.

Finally, even a very efficient SLEP strategy provides only a brief respite and does nothing more than slow the inevitable decline in capabilities and in the value and utility of the Canadian Armed Forces to other government priorities, especially in matters of foreign policy.

The primary challenge of the next administration will be to decide either to provide a capital-renewal budget adequate to maintaining "full-service" defence capabilities or to deliver a clear policy direction to DND as to which capabilities will be maintained. The decision is not so much a choice for the next government as a dilemma with profound implications for foreign policy and national sovereignty.

NOTES

[1]United States Congressional Budget Office, *The Effects of Aging on the Costs of Operating and Maintaining Military Equipment* (Washington, DC: August 2001); http://www.cbo.gov/showdoc.cfm?index=2982&sequence=0#pt2

[2]Statement of Dr. Raymond Pyles, The RAND Corporation, before the Subcommittee on Military Procurement, Committee on Armed Services, U.S. House of Representatives, 24 February 1999.

[3]United States Congressional Budget Office, *The Effects of Aging on the Costs of Operating and Maintaining Military Equipment*.

The Capital and the Future Force Crisis   51

⁴Chris Wattie, "Few Air Force Hercules Can Fly," *The National Post*, 5 July 2003.

⁵Capt Dave Muralt, "Improving Hercules Availability," 2003. http://www.forces.gc.ca/site/feature_story/2003/jul03/21_f_e.asp. 24 July.

⁶Report of Auditor-General of Canada 2001. Chapter 10–National Defence, Exhibit 10-4 - In Service Equipment. Annual Flying Hours by Air Force Fleet; http://www.oagbvg.gc.ca/domino/reports.nsf/html/0110xe04.html

⁷DGPA TRANSCRIPTS. TOPIC: Officials of National Defence will hold a round table briefing on the Maritime Helicopter Program. DATE-TIME: 05 11h00 June 2003, REFERENCE: 03060509.

⁸BGen (retd) Colin Curleigh, "Sea Kings and Recent Sensational Headlines," *Maritime Affairs: The Journal of the Naval Officers' Association of Canada*, 1998.

⁹Report of Auditor-General of Canada 2001. Chapter 10–National Defence, Exhibit 10-5 - Abort rates per 1,000 flying hours, by Air Force fleet; http://www.oagbvg.gc.ca/domino/reports.nsf/html/0110xe05.html

¹⁰Dale Grant, "Godot Flies a Helicopter," *Defence Policy Review*, Vol. 9, No. 9, 9 June 2003.

¹¹Report of Auditor-General of Canada 2001. Chapter 10–National Defence, Exhibit 10-8 – Sea King Serviceability Problems; http://www.oagbvg.gc.ca/domino/reports.nsf/html/0110xe08.html

¹²Statement of Lane Pierrot, Senior Analyst, National Security Division, Congressional Budget Office before the Subcommittee on Military Procurement, Committee on Armed Services, U.S. House of Representatives, 24 February 1999; http://www.cbo.gov/showdoc.cfm?index=1096&sequence=0

¹³Statement of H. Lee Buchanan, Assistant Secretary of the Navy for Research, Development and Acquisition before the Armed Services Committee, House of Representatives, 24 February 1999.

¹⁴"Concerning Readiness," Statement of Lieutenant General Peter Pace, Commander, U.S. Marine Corps Forces, Atlantic, before the National Security Committee, U.S. House of Representatives, 25 September 1998; http://armedservices.house.gov/testimony/105thcongress/98-09-5pace.htm

¹⁵Ibid.

¹⁶The M113A3s, AVGPs, and Bisons have been going through a service life extension project (SLEP), or rebuild. Given that one could expect a service life of 20-30 years for a new vehicle, the SLEP life extension is estimated to be 75 percent of that, or 15-23 years.

[17]Life expectancy is from the 1994 *Report of the Special Joint Committee of the Senate and House of Commons of Canada on Canada's Defence Policy: Security in a Changing World.*

[18]DGPA TRANSCRIPTS, TOPIC: round table briefing on the Maritime Helicopter Program.

[19]Mean of costs reported in FY 2001/2002/2003 DOD Budget Requests in US dollars.

[20]"Family of Medium Tactical Trucks," http://www.ssss.com/fmtv/pdf/tvsbro.pdf

[21]Mean of costs reported in FY 2001/2002/2003 DOD Budget Requests in US dollars.

[22]United States Congressional Budget Office Testimony on Modernizing Tactical Aircraft, before the Subcommittee on Airland Committee on Armed Services United States Senate, 10 March 1999.

[23]Mean of costs reported in FY 2001/2002/2003 DOD Budget Requests in US dollars.

[24]*Defence Plan 2001*, Table 4-3, showed cost estimates of $1.6 billion for Strategic Airlift and $1.62 billion for ALSC, an effective 50/50 split. However, *Federal Procurement of Shipbuilding and Ship Repair Services Overview and Outlook Report of the Senior Officials' Task Force April, 2002 - Procurement Outlook* shows $2.3 billion for the Afloat Logistics and Sealift Capability ships alone; http://strategis.ic.gc.ca/epic/internet/insim-cnmi.nsf/vwGeneratedInterE/uv00018e.html

[25]*Federal Procurement of Shipbuilding and Ship Repair Services.*

[26]"ISTAR Omnibus" presentation by the Directorate of Land Requirements to the Army ISTAR Symposium, 11-12 February 2003, slide 5; http://armyapp.dnd.ca/lfdts/Army_symposium.asp

[27]*Defence Plan On-Line 2002-2003,* Report on Plans and Priorities: Financial Resources - Financial Summary Table, shows LIFEX as a $1.2 billion project, whereas *Federal Procurement of Shipbuilding and Ship Repair Services* shows it as a $2.0 billion project; http://www.vcds.forces.gc.ca/DPOnline/PrioritiesCapitalEquip_e.asp?SelectedDPMenu=4

[28]SELEX is not listed in *Defence Plan On-Line 2002-2003*. Report on Plans and Priorities. The figure here is drawn from *Federal Procurement of Shipbuilding and Ship Repair Services.*

[29]*NATO Facts and Figures*, *NATO Review*, various years.

[30]*Department of National Defence 2003-2004 Report on Plans and Priorities,* 57–58; http://www.vcds.dnd.ca/dgsp/pubs/rep-pub/RPP03-04_E.pdf

[31]"ISTAR Omnibus," slide 5.

[32]Wattie, "Few Air Force Hercules Can Fly." This figure is slightly higher than the estimated cost using the algorithm in Table 4.

[33]The 2002 Long Term Capital Expectations Plan (Equipment) shows an average cost of $302 per vehicle, but the specific vehicle on which this figure is based is not shown. This table uses a more conservative figure based on the US FMTV in Table 4.

[34]This is a "placeholder" figure. It is likely that the M-109 replacement will not be a tracked self-propelled gun, which would be too heavy to be air-lifted as part of the Medium Force concept. While a 120mm breech-loading mortar turret is available for the LAV series of vehicles, its range is substantially less than that of the M-109. A proposal has been made to mount the XM-777 lightweight 155mm howitzer on the LAV chassis, but this is still in the conceptual stage. HIMARS (a smaller version of the highly effective MLRS mounted on a wheeled chassis, which makes it light enough to be air-lifted by a CC-130) is not really suited to be a Close Support artillery system, although it is an excellent General Support system.

[35]Comment by a former Director of Land Requirements that the cost of the turret for the AGS had been estimated at $2.3 million, whereas the basic Stryker chassis estimate was $1.9 million. According to Global Security, the cost of the initial production run of 10 Stryker AGS was US$4.8 million; http://www.globalsecurity.org/military/systems/ground/iav-mgs.htm

[36]This is expressed as "Future Years' Requirements" in the *Reports on Plans and Priorities.*

[37]Government of Canada, Department of National Defence, *1994 Defence White Paper* (Ottawa: Canada Communication Group, 1994), 38.

[38]The 1988 contract cost per vehicle reported in the 1995-96 Estimates was adjusted to an estimated 2003 cost per vehicle, using the US Army Inflation Indices for FY2000 guidance; http://www.amc.army.mil/amc/rm/html/inflation.html

[39]This duplicates the cost of the current LSVW contract award.

[40]A "placeholder guestimate".

[41]This is modelled on the USMC H-1 upgrade at a 2002 cost per aircraft of US$3.2 million, a US$/C$ exchange rate of 1.3368, and a fleet of 100 helicopters, for an upgrade-cost estimate of $4.28 million each, which would represent approximately 33 percent of the original cost of approximately $12.9 million per Griffon.

[42]*Federal Procurement of Shipbuilding and Ship Repair Services.*

[43] This figure is the estimated shortfall in capital availability from the previous period.

[44] Department of National Defence, Report on Plans and Priorities 2001-02, Status of Major Capital Equipment Projects, Armoured Personnel Carrier Replacement Project cost per carrier.

[45] Wattie, "Few Air Force Hercules Can Fly."

[46] The Multi-Mission Maritime Aircraft (MMA) is in the development stage, and costs are not available at this time. The platform-cost figure used is a "placeholder guestimate".

[47] The JSF project is intended to reduce procurement costs per aircraft to the target figure cited. However, the cost per aircraft is likely to be increased because R&D costs are rising and the number of planes likely to be ordered is decreasing. The current flyaway cost of the FA-18E/F is used to get a sense of what might be the upper limit of the JSF flyaway cost.

[48] Modelled as half the sensor update planned for LAV/LAV Recce/Skyguard/ADATS: "ISTAR Omnibus", slide 5.

[49] Modelled on 33 percent of the original platform cost of $1.04 billion.

[50] Modelled on 33 percent of the original project cost of $0.746 billion.

[51] *Defence Plan On-Line 2003-2004*. Report on Plans and Priorities: Financial Resources - Financial Summary Table; http://www.vcds.forces.gc.ca/dponline/prioritiescapitalequip_e.asp?selecteddpmenu=4

CHAPTER THREE

The Personnel Crisis

Christopher Ankersen

The significant hemorrhaging of trained and experienced personnel from the ranks of the military over the last few years has had and will continue to have an impact on readiness for some time to come, given the time and costs involved in bringing new recruits up to similar levels of training and experience.[1]

Facing Our Responsibilities,
Standing Committee on National Defence and Veterans Affairs.
May 2002

THE LIVING ARMED FORCES

In the military system of systems, people are the key to operational effectiveness and thus to the attainment of national defence policy. Even in the age of the so-called Revolution in Military Affairs, attracting, training, employing, and retaining good people are critical functions of armed forces and the mainstay of defence policy. People in the present Canadian Armed Forces are under stress, and the future Canadian Forces is at risk. Whatever the technical advancements that characterize modern armed forces, numbers of people matter. Today, one solider properly equipped and supported may well be capable of doing what three soldiers did just ten years ago, but one soldier cannot be sent to three separate places at the same time or be on continuous, active duty without relief.

Armed forces age, grow weary, and must be rejuvenated if they are to be useful to the nation. Operational duties are the province of young people commanded at all levels by experienced leaders who are promoted on merit gained through active service. Any armed force composed of too many young, inexperienced people is of doubtful utility, as is any force composed of too many senior people. Prudent national defence policy, therefore, must be aimed at maintaining a force with a healthy balance of youth and experience. It must also encourage a system of recruitment, personnel development, and retirement that cultivates a continuous current of people flowing through the ranks year by year. Failures or weaknesses in any of these areas of national policy will invariably be revealed when the system comes under stress, but by then the problem will be beyond immediate remedy.

Citizens cannot be made into soldiers overnight. Recruits cannot be made into fighters in a day, and leaders cannot be produced without the seasoning of experience. Regardless of their individual merits, people cannot be formed into effective operational units without time to train and to rehearse their collective duties. Armed forces learn by doing, and recruits learn their trade from the transfer of experience and from the lessons and the gospel taught by veterans. Break the current or interrupt the flow in any branch of the armed forces, and the follow-on force will, to some degree, wither and lessons will have to be relearned, perhaps at great cost.

The Canadian Forces is on the verge of a personnel crisis, not just of numbers but also of sustainment. As the following figures will illustrate, people of experience are leaving the armed forces early, the recruitment and training systems are erratic, the experience gap is too wide, and as a result, the competence and capabilities of the Canadian Forces may be much reduced.

Leading and managing people, or to use the current de-personified term "Human Resource management", consists, according to the DND Human Resource (HR) "strategic vision" document (HR2020), of five stages: the identification of requirements, recruitment, training and development, employment and deployment, and retirement. Any decision made in any one of these stages may influence, for better or worse, decisions in every other stage. For example, if the HR requirements for recruits are misidentified – set too high or too low, for instance – then training, employment, and retirement policies may be affected.

More important, however, is the basic fact that if the personnel-planners get it wrong, their decision may have significant effects on every other aspect of defence plans and costs and on the operational capabilities of the armed forces as a whole. Experience tells us, moreover, that the effects of personnel decisions tend to flow through the Canadian Forces for years, creating or sustaining problems over a long period. The policy taken in the early 1990s to radically and rapidly "downsize" the armed forces was accomplished in part by severely restricting recruiting. The result was a break in the personnel flow, and that gap is still evident today. When, in the next few years, the older pre-1990s cohort leaves the armed forces, their replacements will be much younger and less experienced than would normally be the case.

Once taken, personnel decisions are difficult to reverse. In the late 1990s, officials and officers decided to let the government-directed force level of 60,000 persons decline to lower levels. That move was intended to find funds for the collapsing capital account. Eventually, the defence minister reversed the decision and restored the 60,000-person establishment, which forced a rapid increase in recruitment that immediately overburdened the training system and drew officers and non-commissioned members from units. Units then suffered for want of leaders.

Any increase in the tempo of overseas operational deployments affects personnel policy and plans, especially if they are unanticipated. Operations in difficult circumstances add to the burden on personnel and tend to reduce the "effective strength" of units as people recover from stress and casualties. These types of operations also increase rates of retirement from the Canadian Forces, which is most worrying when they involve newly recruited and short-service members. This effect increases the pressures on the recruitment and training system and on those experienced members who remain. Unfortunately, increased operational tempo and the unplanned departure of experienced personnel also reduce the number of available and experienced instructors, thereby constraining what could be achieved during any particular development stage. Since fewer instructors means that fewer trainees graduate, many recruits simply become frustrated with the system and leave the military.

Capital-equipment procurements, the location of CF infrastructure, and living conditions on bases, to name but three examples, will also affect the way in which military personnel value their time in the armed forces. If they worry constantly for their safety because they are forced to use old or inadequate vehicles and kit, soldiers may reconsider their line of work. If aircrew are too frequently forced to ask their families to make difficult sacrifices with respect to careers or education because they must return to operational duties, then they may find it in their medium- and long-term interest to opt for a shorter spell in the military than they originally intended.

All these factors are influenced by the world outside the Canadian Forces and especially by the state of the economy. When opportunities exist to find greater job satisfaction and a more stable life, many members of the Canadian Forces who have done their duty leave. The attitude of Canadians and political leaders towards the armed forces can greatly affect morale and decisions to go or stay. Civilian contractors, some of whom have large government defence contracts, regularly hunt down military talent and take service-trained people out of the Canadian Forces. Government departments simply do not seem able to react quickly enough to counter such raiding, and they let well-qualified, and in some cases critical, people walk away. It is strange that any organization would spend millions of dollars recruiting and training people and then let them leave for want of a few hundred dollars in salaries and benefits, but it is a dangerous game when this happens in the Canadian Forces, whose people cannot readily be replaced from the civilian labour pool.

Any discussion of defence policy must address the human challenges facing the Canadian Armed Forces and, in doing so, must answer four basic questions: What is the nature of the current problem? What caused this problem to occur? What are the implications of the problem, in terms of both organizational effectiveness and costs? What can be done?

The answers to these questions reveal a system under severe strain, with sizeable gaps in the personnel strengths and falling levels of quality and experience in critical occupations within the CF. These intertwined problems will be costly to repair. But even if nearly unlimited amounts of money were available, it would take several years to (re)create a personnel system suited to the demands of policy and to rebuild and transform essential occupations under experienced leaders in order to provide a healthy and sustainable armed force for Canada.

Of all the problems confronting personnel managers in the Canadian Forces, two are in the most urgent need of repair: maintaining establishments at full strength and high degrees of competence. The Canadian

Forces simply has too few trained personnel to fulfil the myriad missions and obligations governments have given it. Ships are tied up awaiting crews; aircraft are in need of ground crews and pilots; and many members of the Canadian Forces are deploying to dangerous, demanding missions too soon after returning home from other missions. In 2003, the number of operational waivers – exemptions from the rule that prohibits CF personnel from deploying within 12 months of a previous overseas mission – have increased. Operations in support of ongoing missions – in Bosnia, for instance – and the war on terrorism have created such demands for operational units that the army and the navy have admitted in public that their people are or soon will be pushed to the limit, and perhaps beyond.

The Liberal government's defence policy, *1994 Defence White Paper,* allowed for a regular force of 60,000 personnel on the basis of 1994 demands. This figure represents every person in uniform, including "non-effectives" (members on training or awaiting training; people who are sick or on sick leave, in detention, or on "retirement leave"; and others not fit for normal duty). Since 1998, the number of non-effective personnel on full pay and allowances has increased from 4,000 people in 2000 to more than 10,000 in 2003. It is projected that the difference between paid, full-time military members and trained "effective" military members will remain at about this level for most of this decade. Carrying a disproportionately high number of non-effective members in the Canadian Forces is a commanding, and perhaps crippling, fact of future defence policy. This personnel circumstance is the direct result of increased operational tempo; early retirements; accelerated levels of recruitment caused by the reversal of earlier policy decisions to cut the forces below 60,000, which increased training demands; and routine retirement, which will increase beyond "normal" profiles. If no remedial measures are taken, the overall problem could continue until at least 2012. In other words, even with increased recruiting, the number of "effectives" in the Canadian Forces will continue to fall and then recover more slowly than the number recruited. If operations increase or a prolonged emergency occurs, then the number of effectives will drop accordingly.

The growing imbalance between the total number of CF members (Total Authorized Strength, or TAS) and the number of trained and available members (Trained Effective Establishment, or TEE) is an institutional reality. Moreover, the gap will have long-term consequences for defence policy as the quality and quantity of members available for duty drop. One cannot, for instance, simply hire unit commanding officers or even junior leaders because they must be developed in-house and matured through experience. Unfortunately, the CF cannot meet the quantity demands for full-time trained effective persons, either. Policy demands some 54,500 effective people, but under the currently approved upper manning level of 60,000 less 10,000 non-effectives, this number are not available. Thus the Canadian Forces and defence policy face a chronic personnel deficit of at least 4,000 trained effective people, which only money, recruits, and time can cure. In the meantime, leaders look to "crisis fixes" such as sharing the shortages among classifications, over-tasking the Regular Force, hiring volunteers from the Reserve Force to fill temporarily full-time positions (about 2,000 people in 2003), reenlisting retired personnel, and retaining personnel past their current terms of service to deal with the problems. Table 3.1 shows this personnel-capability gap.

Table 3.1
Personnel Capability Gap (TEE-TES)

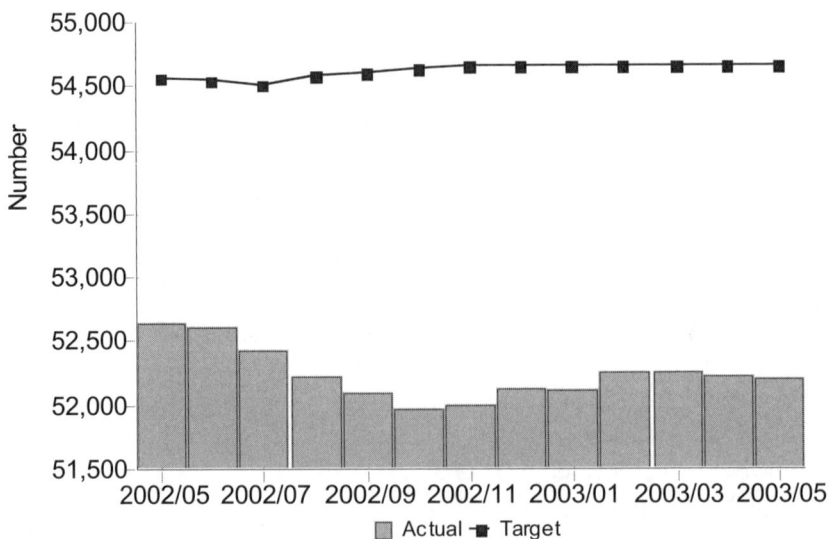

Source: DMC Report.

Officials sometimes assert the Canadian Forces is meeting over 96 percent of its personnel requirements, but this figure does not clearly indicate the effect that the manning shortfall of more than 4,000 trained soldiers, sailors, and airmen and -women is having on the armed forces as a coherent operational entity. Indeed, the problem is so severely debilitating that senior Canadian Forces leaders believe this critical shortfall has severely affected the ability of the Canadian Forces to train and generate forces. The current TEE level of the CF is insufficient to meet operational commitments/tasks.[2]

The numbers problem in the Canadian Forces tells only one side of the personnel story. Quality, as well as quantity, is important in creating a strong and effective military. Ideally, the armed forces would prefer a military population that is balanced among occupational classifications and between junior and senior members. Senior members are valuable not only for their inherent experience, but for their qualities as leaders, mentors, and trainers for the next generation. Therefore, a stable personnel profile would represent a balanced distribution of ages and experience. However, the current population of the Canadian Forces is not stable. The solid line on Table 3.2 represents the current profile of non-commissioned members, but the officer profile is similar.

As the bar graph in Table 3.2 explains, the Canadian Forces' population is seriously skewed in three areas, which are indicated by the bars either well below or well above the line. The portion of the population with 1-4 years of service (YOS) is too large; that with 6-11 YOS is too small; and the portion with 12-18 YOS is also too large. At the 6-11 YOS level of experience, one would expect a non-commissioned member (NCM) to have reached the rank of Master Corporal/Master Seaman to Sergeant/Petty Officer 2nd Class. These people hold key junior-leadership positions, as commanders and supervisors of infantry or naval sections or air-maintenance and flight crews, for example. With insufficient numbers, these key positions often go unfilled or are filled by more junior (i.e. less experienced, perhaps underqualified) personnel. This deficiency will progress through the Canadian Forces as the graph shows, as this cohort or generation, serves out its time in the military. The shortage of sergeants today is propelled into a shortage of qualified warrant officers tomorrow.

Table 3.2
Ideal and Actual Population Distribution (NCM)

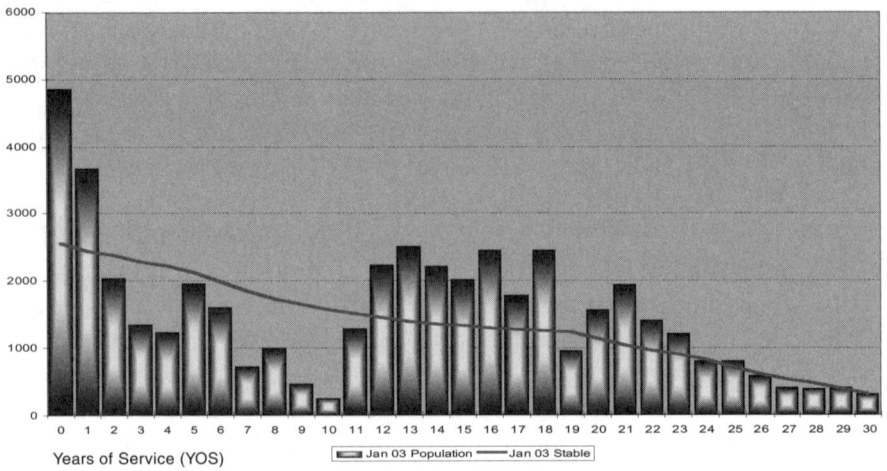

Source: ADM (HR-MIL) Study.

At the 12-18 YOS level, there is a surplus. On the one hand, this might be a good thing if these personnel can help make up for the shortfall in the number of junior leaders. However, as 20 years of service marks a significant exit point for CF members,[3] many members who belong to this cohort might leave within the next two to eight years. This would cause another population dip, further depleting the stock of experienced NCMs.[4] Two such drops in succession would leave the CF virtually denuded of good-quality NCMs to fill second-level NCM positions in operational and technical units and training establishments.

The portion of the population with less than four years of service (Table 3.2 above the stable line) represents those personnel enrolled since 2001, during what might be described as the recruiting blitz.[5] While this increase in personnel may boost the overall numbers of personnel within the CF, other outcomes are likely to be less positive. First, the effect may be short-lived, given that many leave after they complete their first Basic Engagement (3 YOS). Alternatively, if the majority do remain in the CF, they simply constitute another personnel "bubble" requiring inordinate attention as it progresses through the next decade.

The personnel imbalance can be illustrated in another way. Measuring the ratio of junior to senior personnel makes the degree to which the CF population is skewed even more apparent. Again, there is an ideal balance: one senior member (16+ YOS) for every junior member (6-15 YOS), allowing for the right mix of trainees and instructors, leaders and followers, and mentors. Statistically, this ideal balance would be represented by an "hourglass" index of 1.0. The current and projected distribution of experience, as measured by YOS, however, indicates that the ideal hourglass will be distorted by 200 percent over the next ten years. This is demonstrated in Table 3.3, Combat Arms Non-Commissioned Members distribution by Years of Service.

An examination of each occupational classification would reveal that some occupations are more seriously stressed than others. Within the army,

Table 3.3
Army NCM Combat Arms Population

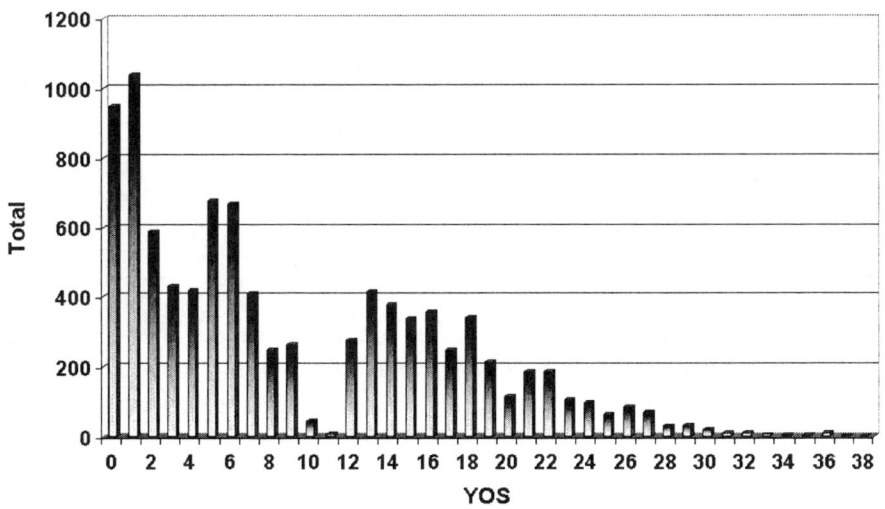

Source: LF AMOR. Peoplesoft information, June 2003 (MOC 011, 021, 022, 031).

for example, the combat classifications are suffering from significant population distortions. There are too many officers with 12-18 years experience, particularly in the Artillery, which means that a large cohort of aging officers is blocking promotions. When young officers see little or no possibility for advancement, they may go to other classifications, take unexpected releases, or at least, leave the CF on completion of their Terms of Service. The abundance of persons with over 12 years of service is anticipated to drive the numbers with 6-11 YOS to new lows in the coming years.

At the NCM level, the story is quite different because there are, and will be, too few senior leaders. (See Table 3.3) As explained above, this means that there are not enough experienced personnel to fill operational positions in units and training establishments. Some positions must go unfilled, but which ones: Instructors at training establishments? Support staff at Reserve units? Junior commanders in operational units? A shortage of instructors is a major contributing factor to the army's inability to complete more than half of its individual training obligations in 2002-2003. The problem is particularly pronounced in field engineer regiments and infantry battalions, where the youngest soldiers are being led by soldiers with not much more experience than their charges.

Across the Canadian Forces, the experience profile of today is significantly different to that of one or two decades ago. Twenty years ago, the CF had a near-ideal balance of adequately trained recruits, experienced leaders, and instructors, as well as a good distribution of long-serving personnel. This more-even, close-to-ideal profile of 1992 has been replaced by a population marked by a shortage of experienced junior leaders and a surplus of new recruits.

WHY DOES THIS PROBLEM EXIST?

The complexity of the military Human Resource system makes it difficult to pinpoint relationships between causes and effects. Many factors contributed to the current state of affairs: demographics of Canadian society, quality of life and other factors affecting retention, the nature of the Terms of Service and the Force Reduction Program of the 1990s, the reversal of some of these policies, and poor recruiting practices generally.

Demographics

Like all western societies, Canadian society is changing. Research into social values has indicated that Canadian society, the pool of potential recruits for the Canadian Forces, is generally concerned with maximizing individual welfare. People are also more suspicious of authority than in other times.[6] The portion of Canadian society traditionally expected to be available for military service (those aged between 16 and 30) holds different values than earlier generations. Adams and Langstaff, relying on Environics data, assert that "Canadians are moving rapidly into a post-modern phase. Our emphasis is shifting toward greater well-being, harmony, and a less traditional quest for spiritual meaning. Canadians, in fact, place greater emphasis on personal freedom and harbour less deference to traditional institutions such as the state, the family, and religious organizations."[7] This situation and these attitudes make it difficult to recruit through traditional themes and challenging to retain people in the military, especially when leaders seem unable to control events and decisions concerning individual well-being.

The state of the Canadian economy at any time is another important factor in military personnel management. When jobs and money are in plentiful in the civilian market, then it is often difficult for the military to attract and retain personnel. Given the favourable Canadian economic situation in the late 1990s, it is little surprise that recruiting levels were low and attrition levels were high. This relationship can affect the Canadian Forces as a whole, or particular classifications as it did through the 1990s in some pilot and air technician trades. Of course, "a sickly season" can have the opposite effect and upset personnel planning when more people than expected suddenly decide to remain in the Canadian Forces past their contracted terms of service. In either case, defence-planners, unlike most civilian employers, are handicapped because they do not have the same degree of flexibility or control over resources (pay and benefits) to adjust terms of service rapidly when external conditions change and competition arises from the civil sector. The significance of this factor is difficult to calculate and even more difficult to predict. Nevertheless, the high degree of interconnectedness between the internal system and externalities is a reality that cannot be changed by defence policy or wished away by hopeful planners. While demographic evolution may be a *cause* of the current personnel crisis, it should not be viewed as an *excuse* for poor planning or inactivity. Clearly, policy must be adjusted to "the facts of national life."[8]

Quality of Life

The Quality of Life factor incorporates a wide range of conditions of employment, including pay and benefits, institutional support provided to people, the sensitivity of leaders to service members' problems that arise from military life, the care of families when members are deployed on operations, and the pace of activity. Many of the problems related to levels of pay during the 1990s have largely been addressed, and pay levels for most rank levels and occupations are competitive with those found in similar civilian careers.

However, if one looks at the pace of activity demanded of CF members, whether due to operational missions or routine tasks within Canada, conditions are unbalanced and are being maintained at an unacceptable and unsustainable level. As Canadian Forces leaders have repeatedly noted, operational tasks in the Balkans and the Middle East, participation in U.S.-led operations at sea and in Afghanistan, as well as the suddenly announced International Security Assistance Force (ISAF) mission in Kabul, have severely taxed military units, particularly those already under the most stress. The common practice now is to "redistribute" people from units at a lower readiness-levels to provide reinforcements to high-readiness and deploying units. At times, entire companies are "borrowed" from one battalion to "round out" another deploying battalion. In the navy, specialist sailors practice "jetty jumping", moving from ship to ship in an effort to make up for shortages in these trades across the fleet. Air crews are also frequently moved or redeployed to fill critical positions overseas. This habit is having significant negative effects on the retention of valuable and expensively trained technical personnel.

Leaders have attempted to limit this practice, partly because of concerns over increasing rates of suicide and divorce in the Canadian Forces in the mid-1990s. The declared policy is that personnel are required to spend 12 months in Canada between deployments to allow time for rest, recuperation, training, and the resumption of a workable home life. The operational requirements of the Canadian Forces, however, remain paramount, and "waivers" exempting personnel from this protection may be signed voluntarily. The number of these waivers is climbing dramatically recently (by over 500 percent, according to sources) and the full effect of Operation Athena – the ISAF deployment to Afghanistan – has yet to be felt. This mission will surely increase personnel dislocations, a conclusion noted by the Chief of the Defence Staff, General Raymond Henault, who candidly warned the government that "the reality of [the Kabul mission] means that we do have very limited ability to take on other missions during that time frame, probably for as much as 18 months after we deploy to Afghanistan with our land force." Lieutenant-General Mike Jeffery, former Chief of the Land Staff, said some time ago that "the mission puts the overall cohesion and sustainability of the army" at risk.

While this deployment policy may control somewhat the pressures to send people on operational assignments, it in no way limits other taskings. Training establishments in the CF do not have enough permanent staff to meet their requirements, and therefore rely on personnel temporarily assigned from other units to fill these roles. A sergeant, for example, could return from a six-month tasking in Afghanistan and then immediately be required to leave home again for several months to instruct on a course at the Combat Training Centre or the Recruit School. While not required to deploy in harm's way, this sergeant is effectively assigned to an internal deployment, with much the same effect on his or her quality of life as an overseas deployment.

If one looks at the total amount of time that Canadian Forces personnel spend away from home on duty, the full dimensions of the problem become starkly evident. The combined tempo of operational and routine tasks in the Canadian Forces during the summer period (the busiest time for training-related tasks) shot up in 2003 to over 4.5 times the level of just three years ago.[9] Again as senior leaders have reported, "Force employment has come at the cost of force generation. Current force employment/commitment levels limit force re-generation capacity. Sustained high levels and duration of operational, individual and general tasks are placing unacceptable burdens on personnel."[10]

In addition to the specific challenges raised by inadequate compensation for hours worked and for a high level of personal dislocation, the fact is that people want to do valuable work and feel appreciated for doing it. Recent reports from the Land Force Command indicate that people are not necessarily being appreciated today.[11] This perception greatly affects the morale of individuals and units, and when the effect is sufficiently negative, many members become frustrated. It can be expected that some will convert this frustration into a "vote with their feet", and leave the Canadian Forces. Often there is little officers can do to remedy this problem because the source of the perception that the Canadian Forces and the work done by its members are not appreciated lies at the centre of government.

Terms of Service and the Force Reduction Program (FRP)

According to Canadian Forces demographers, the single biggest factor influencing retention is Terms of Service (TOS), i.e., the parameters of the employment contract detailing how long members must serve, the size of the pension they are eligible for, etc.[12] If the incentives exist for service members to stay, they will stay. If the TOS favour a member's early release, he/she will go. As a result, it is critical for the CF to get the details of the TOS correct because they have a lasting and significant impact on force levels. Planners, therefore, have attempted to make TOS both more appealing and more restrictive, so as to reduce incentives to leave. For example, the Compulsory Retirement Age (CRA) has been changed from 55 to 60 years of age, and more members have been given "intermediate" and "indeterminate" contracts. On the other hand, members are no longer allowed to leave the Canadian Forces before completing the full terms of their service contracts.

It is questionable, however, whether these changes will have any lasting effect. For example, on average less than 1 percent of the CF population and only 8 percent of the annual total releases from the military include CF personnel who actually completed their terms of service. By far the largest number of releases are "unscheduled," resulting from training failures, disciplinary cases, medical requirements, and other causes. That the majority of annual releases, 92 percent, are unscheduled serves as an indicator of the instability, the high degree of unpredictability, in the personnel system. Both these factors are cause for concern, but no reliable policy response has so far been made to rectify either of them.

In the 1990s, a concerted effort was made to reduce rapidly the strength of the Canadian Forces by offering "incentive" packages to individuals. This policy, made in response to the draw-downs called for in *1994 Defence White Paper*, was known as the Force Reduction Program (FRP). Attractive incentives were offered to senior NCMs and officers and, not surprisingly, attrition rose sharply (from 6 to 12 percent) as officers and senior NCMs (many already eligible for annuities) signed up for the early-out program. Since little effort was made to restrict the departure of mission-sensitive members, many people who were or soon would be in demand left, taking with them years of valuable experience. The reduction program was accelerated, restricting recruiting in several Military Occupation Classifications (MOCs). These twin policies had the double effect of chopping two ends – the older, experienced portion and the younger replacement portion – from the personnel stream. The effects of these policies, moreover, are now travelling through the Canadian Forces and are evident in the population profiles of the armed forces.

Weak Recruiting Practices

The CF is constrained in how it can address the issue of personnel replacement. It cannot hire laterally, as the private and public sectors can. Military personnel management must follow the order laid out in the theoretical life cycle described above. Recruiting, therefore, is the only way to bring new personnel into the Canadian Forces. As we have already seen, however, recruiting large numbers of people is not always a viable, sustainable, long-term solution to the people problems. Some may see throwing open the recruiting doors, as is being done in 2003, as a "quick fix", but it may create other negative and unintended consequences. When, for example, the navy faced a critical personnel shortfall, large numbers of sailors were recruited. Unfortunately, most of the shortages were in technical trades, but to keep the numbers up, many of the personnel recruited were unsuitable for these highly skilled, specialist trades and were assigned to the more general "Boatswain" occupation. Today, the Boatswain trade has a surplus at the junior-leader rank levels, while the technical trades are still under strength. Furthermore, once the surplus was noted within the Boatswain trade, general naval recruiting was halted, creating a new shortage in the number of entry-level Boatswains. These types of stop-start reactions contribute to the creation of "bubbles" and "dips" in population profiles, causing turmoil in the personnel system for years into the future.

This example illustrates how mistakes made during the recruiting phase can lead to severe consequences that are difficult to manage and even harder to correct later. By focussing on recruiting as the sole quick-fix, the Canadian Forces does itself a disservice. Retaining the personnel already in the service (and maintaining a population profile close to the ideal) is a sounder strategy. In fact, the costs associated with recruiting, especially in training and attrition can easily wipe out limited gains made through increased recruiting. For a number of reasons, as we shall discuss in subsequent sections of this chapter, retention is key.[13] Or by way of analogy, it is better to seal the leaking bucket than to waste endless effort trying to keep it full.

THE NATIONAL DEFENCE IMPLICATIONS OF THE PERSONNEL CRISIS

The preceding sections spelled out the extent of the personnel crisis, but the critical question remains: so what? Five key implications arise from the current personnel situation within the CF: training difficulties, human resource management challenges, deepening retention problems, a reduction in operational effectiveness, and the significant amount of money that the personnel crisis is costing the Canadian Forces.

Training Difficulties

As discussed above, the largest proportion of instructors within the Canadian Forces consists of "incremental staffs": personnel serving in units and other locations who are temporarily tasked in a training establishment. As the number of experienced officers and NCMs changes, the availability of instructors varies. A shortage of instructors means that more junior personnel are often tasked to fill in when more appropriate instructors are not available, and that many positions are filled by a shrinking pool of potential instructors who are required to teach more often and for longer periods. Since this effect means that incremental instructors will be away from their usual home units for longer periods, personal dislocations increase, exacerbating the problems associated with a randomly dislocated life, especially for married members.

Fewer instructors usually means fewer and smaller training courses, which is at variance with the demand to train large numbers of new recruits and junior personnel who need advanced qualifications if they are to fill in behind the older cohort. The Years of Service profile of the Canadian Forces NCM population (illustrated in Table 3.2) shows a dramatic increase in the number of personnel with 0-3 YOS, and they all need to be trained. As recruiting targets will continue at an elevated level for several years, the demand for training will necessarily remain high. Bottlenecks in the system are already a fact of life, forcing new entrants to wait for courses, often while performing boring or menial tasks in the meantime. As this practice increases, it will have a negative effect on retention. These bottlenecks also mean that career and leadership courses for personnel already in the system are delayed or deferred. This consequence not only causes retention problems but also may lower the quality of this portion of the population, as well as their readiness and availability to assume greater responsibility in the future as older members reach their compulsory retirement age.

An additional training difficulty occurs as a result of attrition among those personnel with 6-15 YOS. In some cases, experienced personnel leave just as they become valuable to the military. This places a double burden on the training system as it struggles to develop these personnel, only to suddenly and unexpectedly have to train a replacement. The problem is particularly acute in Maritime Surface/Sub-Surface (MARS) officer classifications. It can take in excess of seven years for these officers to reach the stage in their careers where they become "directors" – fully qualified officers who run the various departments on a ship. By the time officers become directors, many have only a few years remaining in service before they may leave the Canadian Forces with a cash bonus for completing their contract. Table 3.4 shows that in the MARS classification, the TES gap at the Lt(Naval) rank is only 9 percent. However, the final column illustrates that if the number of Lt(N)s who are not directors is factored in, the real deficit is over 20 percent.

Table 3.4
MARS TEE-TES Gap, Highlighting the Shortage of Directors

	Capt (N)	*Cdr*	*LCdr*	*Lt(N)/SLt*	*Lt(N)/SLt (Directors)*
TEE (Establishment)	42	110	284	448	448
TES (Strength)	35	105	256	407	354
Difference	-7	-5	-28	-41	-94
TEE filled (%)	83%	95%	90%	91%	79%

While the overall size of the MARS-officer deficit may be manageable, the fact that there are many vacancies at the director level indicates that numbers are not the sole problem. Rather, the loss of critical expertise caused by failures of personnel policy is the truly significant current and future operational problem. As we have seen, the quantitative and qualitative aspects of personnel issues cannot be easily separated.

Training Production: Meeting the Trained Effective Establishment

Increased recruiting not only puts pressure on a small instructor pool, but also affects the total number of personnel who can be taken on effective strength. When people enroll, they are placed on what is called the Basic Training List (BTL) until they receive their recruit and basic occupational training. This training phase varies according to whether the enrollees are officers or NCMs, the specific occupation into which they will be deployed, and as discussed above, the availability of course vacancies. The length of time a person may spend on the BTL is about two years for an NCM and between two and five years for an officer.

The effect of adding a person to the BTL depends on the flexibility permitted with respect to the Total Paid Strength (TPS)[14] of the Canadian Forces. In a situation where TPS is allowed to vary, one more person is added to the payroll, even though that individual cannot be counted as a trained, effective member of the armed forces. If TES targets are to be met under these conditions, the TPS must increase above the Total Authorized Strength level of 60,000 personnel, as shown in Table 3.5. When this policy is in effect, costs rise and financial pressure on the total defence budget increases. Given that the funding "vote", or allocation for personnel, is based on a strength of 60,000 people, there can be no automatic accommodation or cash for any personnel strength above 60,000.

On the other hand, if the TPS restricts the personnel strength to the authorized level of 60,000 personnel, the effect of adding a person to the BTL is more severe because it limits the number of trained effective personnel who can be accommodated. In other words, in this zero-sum situation, the TPS and the BTL must be in balance. In this scenario, the longer a person remains on the BTL, the longer the effectiveness of the CF remains depressed. The ratio of those on the BTL to those actually trained and transferred to the TES varies by entry-programme, but in all cases it is greater than 2 to 1.[15]

Table 3.5
Required Total Paid Strength versus Total Authorized Strength

Year	2000/01	2001/02	2002/03	2003/04	2004/05	2005/06
Required TPS	58,852	59,251	61,432	62,150	62,250	62,450
TAS	60,000	60,000	60,000	60,000	60,000	60,000
% TAS	98.1%	98.7%	102.4%	103.6%	103.8%	104.1%

The swelling of the BTL to accommodate increased recruiting is causing the mix of officer-entry plans to be re-evaluated. Officers who enrol with degrees are designated Direct Entry Officers (DEO) and spend only two years on the BTL. Those officers who attend The Royal Military College or are sponsored in their undergraduate education are part of the Regular Officer Training Plan (ROTP) and spend five years on the BTL. The implications of this difference are significant, especially in a situation where the authorized strength of the Canadian Forces cannot be exceeded. CF demographers believe that a decrease in the annual enrolment of ROTP and an increase in DEO recruiting by 300 personnel would increase the TES by 900 personnel. But this solution seems out of reach.

Canadian Forces human resource modelling illustrates the situation dramatically.[16] Given that the ROTP is the principal means of officer enrolment, it is not likely to be discontinued in favour of the DEO program. Therefore, under these assumptions and even if the TPS were allowed to exceed the authorized strength of 60,000 people, the CF could not reach TEE until 2012. Even under best-case assumptions regarding recruiting targets and following projected attrition rates, this analysis means that a fully trained and effective military is at least a decade in the offing. In this optimistic scenario, the CF would be under considerable budgetary pressures as it tried to fund an additional 2,500 personnel to facilitate this production model.

If the TPS is not permitted to exceed 60,000, then the situation is far worse. In this event, then even in the unlikely case that ROTP enrolments are eliminated and that lower than expected attrition rates are consistently achieved, the Canadian Forces could not reach its TEE until after 2030. These startling projections highlight another key aspect of interdependencies within the personnel system. There are no cheap, quick fixes. Every suggestion for correcting the personnel crisis must be tracked well into the future to avoid importing into that era problems caused by trying to manage current difficulties with short-term fixes.

HUMAN RESOURCE MANAGEMENT CHALLENGES

One of the most frustrating aspects of the Hourglass Experience Index imbalance is succession planning. At an Hourglass Index of 1.0, succession planning (including promotion forecasting and career development) is a simple matter: as experienced members of the population advance or retire, replacements can be identified in the slightly larger, less experienced cohort behind them. For example, let's assume Cohort X provides commanding officers (COs) for eight air force squadrons. Those eight members of Cohort X will complete their command tours; some will be promoted, some will move laterally, and some will choose to leave the CF. In this way, Cohort X gets smaller over time. Meanwhile, in order to manage the need to find eight new commanding officers, one need only look to the more junior, but somewhat larger, Cohort Y. Ideally, it would be possible to identify more than eight potential candidates, prepare them for command and promote some of them. In the end, choosing eight COs would be a matter of selecting the best people from Cohort Y.

If, however, the cohorts do not follow the ideal profile, succession planning is not as straightforward. If Cohort X is too large, it may be necessary to find worthwhile employment for those not chosen for command and for those progressing past that milestone. Without a degree of manageable attrition, the problem becomes one of occupying people's time with meaningful and valuable work. If, on the other hand, Cohort Y is too small, it becomes difficult to find enough properly qualified personnel to fill important positions. Either these positions must go vacant, or less capable individuals have to be employed.

A final problem of human resource management is the temptation for managers to opt for short-term solutions to fix immediate and pressing problems. The case of the surplus Boatswains (discussed above) illustrates the results of this practice. Other examples of this habit can be seen in the combined effects of the shortage of director-level officers in the navy and the high BTL-to-production ratio posed by ROTP entrants. To satisfy the need to produce more director-level officers, there is a tendency to "go for the high school grad" in lieu of an ROTP entrant. Non-degreed officers are more immediately available for employment, but in light of current policy, which states that all officers shall have at least an undergraduate education, they will require significant educational "top-up" sometime during their careers. While such a preference may appear to solve an immediate issue, it may ultimately cause a more serious one later on. What good is it recruiting non-degreed officers, if down the road in their careers, they will need further education or face restrictions in employment and promotion?

Deepening Retention Problems

Predictably, one of the most significant implications of the personnel crisis is its compound nature. As shortages become critical, the need for additional instructors rises, increasing levels of personnel dislocation. This fact has already been identified as having a negative effect on attrition rates. Furthermore, taking more personnel away from their units to act as instructors means that other, less qualified, personnel may have to pick up the slack. Of course, the workload in units is already higher than normal due to the shortages in personnel, which is the cause of the increased instructor bill in the first place! In this situation, however, the problem is merely shifted from one unit, the training establishment, to another, the operational unit. It is a classic case of robbing Peter to pay Paul, and it is no solution at all.

The effect of constrained succession planning may be that incompetent or inexperienced people occupy leadership positions. Working for, and perhaps compensating for, such leaders may also lead to high levels of frustration and dissatisfaction in units, including those in the field and at sea, with the possibility of serious disciplinary and operational consequences in units under stress. All these related effects may also significantly accelerate attrition, which further exaggerates and compounds the personnel crisis.

Reduction in Operational Effectiveness

The bottom line in the military is operational effectiveness; results matter when a field engineer troop is conducting mine-clearance overseas, when an aircraft is conducting search and rescue operations in bad weather, or when a ship is crossing a difficult stretch of ocean. With fewer people, some of whom may be underqualified for the jobs they hold, the ability to meet demanding standards posed by operations is jeopardized. In a few words, capabilities are eroded, and some may collapse entirely and in very inappropriate and dangerous circumstances.

Not surprisingly, it is the operational classifications that are most affected by the personnel crisis. People in operational units in all capability fields tend to have the highest operational tempo in the least attractive circumstances and to suffer the greatest long-term post-traumatic stress. Consequently, their attrition rates follow suit. The examples are sobering: the MARS officer classification is currently 10 percent below TES, with less than the minimal operational level of directors; 75 percent of infantry soldiers leave by the end of their first three years of service. With releases in key occupational groups set to exceed historical levels by 150 percent, there can be no doubt as to the gravity of the situation. As the operational units of the Canadian Armed Forces go, so goes Canada's national defence.

Cost

DND has struggled with various approaches to costing individual training and education (IT&E), but has run into challenges as people move from one Managing Authority (MA) to another and as MAs move resources from one accounting system to another. The result is that there is no reliable way to determine the costs of IT&E in the Canadian Forces. A useful attempt to understand costs was made between 1997 and 2000, using an independent analysis of a one-year time frame and tracing costs across MAs.[17] Tables 3.6 and 3.7 record the total amounts spent by MAs and accounting systems.

The tables record total costs observed in one year for all training for all Regular Force personnel (Recruit to commanding officer, i.e., LCol / Cdr). As the current challenge for the CF is to restore the first 20 years of experience, only Development Periods (DP) One and Two (individual training from Recruit to Major) are included in this cost analysis. By adding together all CF classification training costs, one can determine that 68 percent of officers' training and 90 percent of NCMs' training occur in DP1 and DP2. (See Tables 3.8 and 3.9.)

Table 3.6
IT&E Costs by Managing Authority, 1997/1998

Managing Authority	Training Days	Cost ($ millions)
Maritime	289,700	288
Army	376,210	736
Air Force	201,090	380
HR(Mil)	589,090	503
Others	110,099	70
Total	**1,567,080**	**1,977**

Table 3.7
IT&E CF Totals, 1997/1998 (Rough Order of Magnitude +/-10%)

Account	Cost ($ millions)
Cost of Personnel in IT&E	481
Cost of Students	248
O&M	410
Capital (Equipment & Infrastructure)	251
Support	587
Total	**1,977**

Since NCMs tend to receive a larger portion of individual training earlier in their careers than officers, the costs of training officers and NCMs cannot be simply averaged. The ratio of officers to NCMs in the CF is approximately 1:4. Therefore, taking 80 percent of the cost of training NCMs (92 percent) plus 20 percent of the cost for officers (68 percent) provides a more accurate reflection of total DP1 and DP2 costs for IT&E.

Table 3.8
CF Officer Occupations: Cost per Development Period
(average of all classifications)

Development Period	IT&E Cost	Days (CF avg.)	Ranks	Remarks
DP1	$243,334		OCdt to Capt	46% of total
DP2	112,772		Capt to Major	22% of total
DP3 A &B	168,222		Major to LCol	
Totals	**$524,776**	**427 days**		

Table 3.9
CF NCM Occupations: Cost per Development Period
(average of all classifications)

Development Period	IT&E Cost	Days (CF avg.)	Ranks	Remarks
DP1	$212,113		Pte to Cpl	47% of total
DP2	196,000		MCpl to Sgt	43% of total
DP3 A &B	45,024		WO to MWO	
Totals	**$453,264**	**339 days**		

By this calculation, the CF annual expenditure for DP1 and DP2 training in 1997/98 was 88 percent of $1.977 billion, or $1.740 billion.

In 1997/98, the intake of the training system was 2,600. Personnel on the BTL and the Advanced Training List (ATL) did not exceed 4,000, and the total annual cost was $1.74 billion. At a time when the CF is taking in 5,000 recruits per year and has a BTL and ATL of over 8,000, one would expect IT&E costs to reflect a proportionate increase (i.e., a doubling) to $3.5 billion, *assuming that savings of scale can be achieved.*

This analysis suggests that an additional $1.5 billion a year must be added to the defence budget for IT&E for each of the next ten years if the personnel deficit is to be eliminated.

WHAT CAN BE DONE?

Three key actions should be taken soon to address the mounting personnel crisis within the greater CF system. They are drastic measures, but as the evidence in this chapter has illustrated, the CF has entered drastic times, and if nothing substantial is done, then the capabilities of the Canadian Forces will rapidly collapse in kind, quantity, and quality.

1. *The total authorized strength of the CF should be incrementally increased to 85,000, or else a significant permanent reduction in operational taskings must be made.* The operational activity level and the internal tasking level indicate that there are too few members in those classifications that are most in demand. Comparing CF personnel and operational activity levels in 1994 to operational activity levels in 2004 implies that a force establishment of 85,000 would be appropriate. If the CF personnel strength is held at 60,000, then the following policies should be brought into force.

2. *The Individual Training and Education system funding must be increased by approximately $1.5 billion.* The current IT&E system is under-resourced for a Total Authorized Strength of 60,000. Restoring the IT&E system should take priority over every other activity. Otherwise, given current trends, the CF Total Effective Strength will drop to about 45,000 by 2010.

3. **Given the skewed distribution of personnel in the CF, the paid ceiling must be raised to or above 62,500 for several years to restore and sustain the trained establishment objective of 54,500.** This means increasing the Total Authorized Strength and funding this difference.

NOTES

[1] Canada, Standing Committee on National Defence and Veterans Affairs. *Facing Our Responsibilities: The State of Readiness of the Canadian Forces*, chapter 6 (Ottawa: Minister of Supply and Service, May 2002), 7.

[2] CF, "Strategic Performance Measurement, First Quarterly Report", 24 June 2003.

[3] Given current Terms of Service, completing 20 years of service entitles a member to retire with an immediate annuity.

[4] While this example used the NCM profile, the officer profile displays the same trends.

[5] See Jonathan Gatehouse and Stewart Bell, "Military launches image offensive to refill its ranks," www.nationalpost.com, 6 January 2001; and Mike Blanchfield, "Military faces recruitment crisis: official," www.globeandmail.com, 6 January 2001.

[6] See Christopher Ankersen, "Leading Individuals and Collectives: Perspectives and Challenges," Canadian Forces Leadership Institute Discussion Paper, 2002. See also L. Wong, "Generations Apart: Xers and Boomers in the Officer Corps," October 2000; http://carlislewww.army.mil/usassi/ssipubs/pubs2000/apart/apart.pdf (accessed 2 July 2001). See also J. Tesseron, "Military Manning and the Revolution in Social Affairs," *Canadian Military Journal* 2.3 (Autumn 2001): 53-62.

[7] M. Adams and A. Langstaff, "You say paternal, and I say relax," *The Globe and Mail* Monday, 3 July 2000; http://erg.environics.net/news/default.asp?aID'409 (accessed July 2, 2001).

[8] For an example of a "throw up your hands" approach to a strong economy, see Col. Gordon Grant, "Manning Issues for the New Millennium: Shaping a Comprehensive Recruiting and Retention Strategy for the Canadian Forces," *CISS Strategic Datalink* No. 97, 2001.

[9] CF "Strategic Performance Measurement, First Quarterly Report," 24 June 2003.

[10] Ibid.

[11] David Pugilese, "Soldiers 'frustrated' by rules, policies," *The Ottawa Citizen*, 23 June 2003.

[12] ADM (HR-Mil) Operational Analysis Study.

[13] See C.P. Ankersen and L. Tethong, "Retain or Perish: Why Recruiting Won't Save the CF," CISS Strategic Datalink #95, 2001; and C.P. Ankersen and L. Tethong, "Birds in Hand: The Need for a Retention Based Strategy for the CF," *Canadian Military Journal* 2.2 (2001): 43-49.

[14]The TPS is made up of the TES+BTL+some other categories, including the SPHL; 97 percent of the TPS is comprised of the TES+BTL. Source: ADM (HR-Mil) Study.

[15]The shortest time on BTL is two years; MARS candidates can be on BTL for six years. This ratio is derived using person-years. The concept can be illustrated by comparison to the medical profession: in order to generate 5,000 doctors a year, 35,000 medical students must annually receive medical training. A similar dynamic exists within the military.

[16]ADM (HR-Mil) Study.

[17]CF TOS Study Phase 3B (August 2000), based on ADGA audit of Individual Training and Education (IT&E) of fiscal year 1997/98.

CHAPTER FOUR

The Gathering Defence Policy Crisis

Howie Marsh

We are going to be limited in our ability to provide any sizeable land force contribution elsewhere on the international scene for the 12 months ... [after the Afghan deployment ends in 2004][1]

General Raymond Henault

THE LIMITS OF RISK MANAGEMENT

The recent history of the Canadian Armed Forces and defence policy is a story of risk management. Unfortunately, the risks will shortly become unmanageable and crisis management will soon replace risk management, not only in defence policy but also in foreign policy and in military responses to domestic emergencies. Since the mid-1980s, successive Canadian governments have provided ever-decreasing expenditure allocations to defence policy, while maintaining, rhetorically at least, an activist international dimension to Canada's foreign policy. This perennial theme has undermined successive defence policies and plans and created various "commitment-capability gaps" – more is pledged in declarations than is made available in fact.[2]

Canadian Forces resources of people, equipment, and logistical support are now so modest that the members of the armed forces struggle to meet the ever-increasing operational tempo required of Canada's defence and foreign policies. What is most worrisome about this contradiction, evident since at least 1987, is that it now heralds the approach of a long season of negligible military capability, perhaps even the collapse of some core capabilities. The gathering crisis is not simply about the loss of these capabilities, but about the effects of this loss on the larger issues of national sovereignty, independent foreign policy, support to the United Nations, and all aspects of relations with the United States in a world of fierce security challenges.

The approaching crisis in military capabilities is the result of the failure of governments to adequately maintain and renew core capabilities and personnel strengths in the Canadian Forces in the face of obvious threats and the demands of operations in the 1990s. The collapse of the "future force" will soon define Canadian defence and foreign policies in ways that will surprise political leaders and the public in general. Recovering from this situation will take many years and large expenditures. In the meantime, the government and its diplomats will be forced to find, if they can, innovative ways to defend and advance Canada's interests and responsibilities in the international community.

Examples of this crisis are already at hand. In the spring of 2003, the defence minister announced that it will be at least a year before the navy can send a ship to join a standing commitment to the NATO fleet. At the April session of NATO's Military Committee, Canada's Chief of Defence Staff alerted his colleagues to the fact that [the Kabul mission] "means that [Canada would have a] very limited ability to take on other missions during that time frame, probably for as much as 18 months after we deploy to Afghanistan with our land force". In a forthright public statement at his change of command parade in June 2003, Lieutenant-General Mike Jeffery, former Chief of the Land Staff, declared that the International Security Assistance Force (ISAF) mission in Kabul places "the overall cohesion and sustainability of the army" at risk.

Military capabilities are produced from four intertwined components: trained personnel, appropriate equipment, unit training, and enablers (maintenance, spare parts, infrastructure, logistical support, etc.). What is alarming (or should be to governments) is the evident fact that virtually every core capability is failing in at least two of these common components. The previous chapters describe the state of major equipment and the state of personnel policy in the Canadian Forces. This chapter exposes the critical deficiencies in the training system and the enablers. But first, the four essential systems need to be set in the context of the major determinants that shape the Canadian military condition.

MAJOR DETERMINANTS OF THE GATHERING CRISIS

The inertia that characterizes every defence institution and all policies is an aspect of national defence policy particularly relevant to the approaching crisis. Like a large flywheel, it will rotate for a long time before it stops. But once it stops, a great deal of energy, time, and money is required to get it moving again.³

Canada's military capabilities, once very significant, declined slowly throughout the Cold War era, but very serious retrenchments began around 1964 under the Liberal government of Mike Pearson. Indeed, the decline continued in the 1960s and then in the 1970s under Pierre Trudeau, when some major capabilities were eliminated entirely. By the early 1980s, the rustout of the Canadian Forces was so pronounced and allied criticism so loud that the matter became a major issue during the 1983 election.

The Mulroney government failed to live up to its election promises on defence policy, saved in part by the end of the Cold War. But the government was not shy about offering depleted units for war operations in the former Yugoslavia or the Persian Gulf. The Canadian Armed Forces were pruned again in the 1990s by the Liberal government, which provided just enough support to its defence policy to sustain the "present force", mostly at the expense of the "future force" (see Historical Annex).

Governments have managed this decline by understating requirements, taking risks, and controlling military activities in the ironically peaceful and predictable Cold War period. That luxury has passed. Today, the Canadian Forces is heavily engaged in real operations, the consequences of which cannot readily be calculated, even from day to day. The demand for forces and capabilities now trumps the government's ability to control activities and costs or to manage risks. Nevertheless, the government has been content to eat into capital funds to support current operations and to live off the avails of the present stock of military resources and the dedication of the few members of the Canadian Forces repeatedly put on the front line. This strategy has now run its course and has propelled Canada into the present crisis in national policy. Reversing this downwards momentum without a change of attitude among Canada's political community will be most difficult.

Time is the master of this process, even more than money. In the 1990s, the Canadian Forces lost approximately 500,000 person-years of experience through normal and forced attrition. Qualified, experienced personnel – such as military engineers, command and intelligence staff officers, and technical specialists in all branches – were let go, and it will take years to recover from this situation. Developing a junior leader can take five to eight years of training and experience, and more than 15 to 20 years are required to develop a unit commander.

Acquiring equipment and bringing it to operational standards require a minimum of 8 to 12 years under present assumptions. Even the seemingly straightforward project to replace combat clothing started in 1992 and was not completed by 2002. More complicated acquisitions like the Unmanned Aerial Surveillance Target Acquisition System (UASTAS) commenced in 1974 and might be partially satisfied in 2004. A replacement for the Sea King Maritime Helicopters was decided before 1983 and then cancelled after 1993. The actual replacement of the maritime-helicopter capability is still at least a decade away, and the new fleet may not be operational until 2013.[4] The Canadian Forces has lost so much momentum in core areas that bringing major capabilities to a full operational state is likely to take one or two decades.

The Minister of National Defence recently announced that the government would proceed with the procurement of the army Intelligence, Surveillance, Target Acquisition, and Reconnaissance system (ISTAR), which is a welcome development.[5] However, nothing of real substance will happen until the main acquisition contract is signed and the prime contractor publishes dates for equipment delivery and schedules for training conversion. At the present time, fielding and initial training on the army ISTAR are planned to occur in 2010-2013 – assuming, of course, that DND can secure capital funds, which seems doubtful.[6]

Every defence White Paper is printed with good intentions, but many of these intentions fail to materialize for want of money and political persistence and oversight of the defence establishment. Delays in making choices, changed and changing priorities within the armed forces, unexpected international events, and domestic concerns interrupt the purposeful flow of military renewal and transformation. The approaching crisis of capabilities is bounded on one side by the state of today's capabilities and on the other by the time it will take to restore, replace, or transform them. Yet as each day passes without decisions to act, the span widens and the crisis deepens.

The Canadian Forces is on the verge of a population collapse. Table 4.1 illustrates the Canadian Forces Regular Force population by Years of Service. If those in the 12-19 YOS "bulge" leave early, they can be replaced only by the 4-11 YOS group, who are few in number and short on experience. Close to 25,000 service members are eligible for early retirement this decade, and they will closely monitor government attitudes and actions in matters of national defence. If they are dissatisfied or overstressed by unreasonable demands, then this cohort may vote with their feet. They will leave in their place the next generation, which not only lacks experience but can provide less than half the number of people required to sustain the extant defence structure. Serving members will need to be convinced by the next government that the Canadian Armed Forces has a meaningful future.

Table 4.1
CF Population by Years of Service

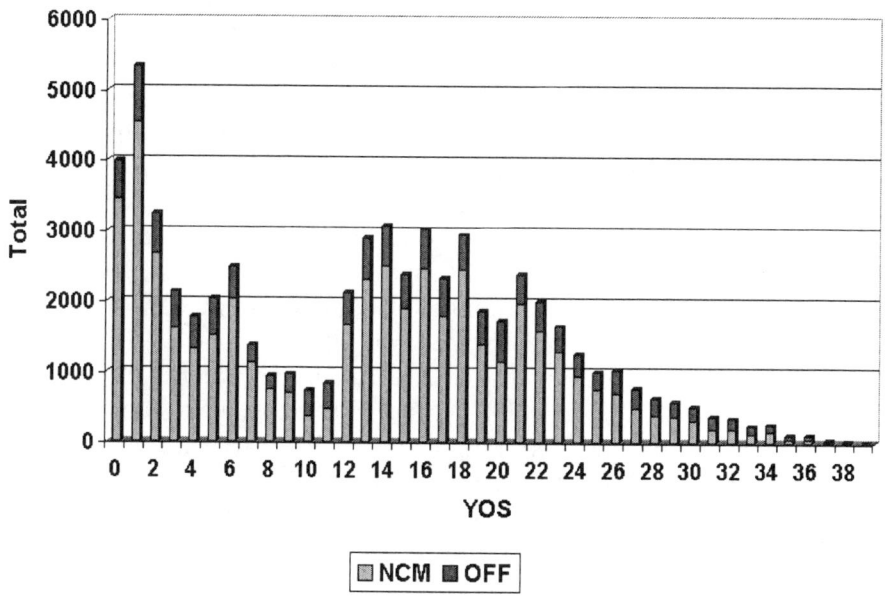

Source: Peoplesoft information, June 2003.

SUPPORTING INTERNATIONAL OPERATIONS

The end of the Cold War removed many of the restraints on international behaviour, leading to regional conflicts, national upheavals, ethnic clashes, and genocide. Canada joined the so-called "International Community" and intervened in various ways in some of these situations. Unfortunately for the Canadian Forces, just as the need for help increased, Canadians leaders began to cut into military capabilities.

The costs of both international operations and more routine duties have increased each year. These costs were absorbed in part by attempts (following a government-wide policy) "to do more with less", the negative effects of which have been well described in various parliamentary documents and in such non-public assessments as *A Nation at Risk,* published by the Conference of Defence Associations.[7]

The policy forced people in the operational classifications, and especially the junior and senior leaders in units, to work an inordinate amount of overtime and spend much of their summers and weekends away from home. But to soldiers, "doing more with less" means, as they say to each other today, "spending soldiers' lives to save taxpayers' money."

The cost of operations was also absorbed by transferring funds meant for capital investment to the O&M account. The O&M budget provides "housekeeping" funds to operate equipment and maintain infrastructure and for transportation and a wide range of other services. The total cost is about $4 billion annually. As activities increase, O&M costs increase also, but they tend to rise fastest when the Canadian Forces is engaged in real operations in faraway places where local support and resources are nearly non-existent, as in Afghanistan. The higher the cost, the more funds must be transferred between accounts; the capital budget is the most flexible but, as a matter of policy, only in the short term.

"Full Cost" accounting for salaries, equipment depreciation, and consumables, as described in DND Main Estimates, makes a good indicator of levels of military activity. As Table 4.2 illustrates, activity levels have fluctuated throughout the period, but the trend is upwards and climbing steeply in 2003. The units most often deployed – army manoeuvre units, major naval combatants, air tactical lift and tactical aviation units, and command and field logistics elements – are also the most expensive to maintain in the field and at sea. They are also the primary and collective capabilities most needed for future operations. As they are used up in

Table 4.2
Cost of Peace and Stability Operations, 1993-2004 (2003/04 Dollars)

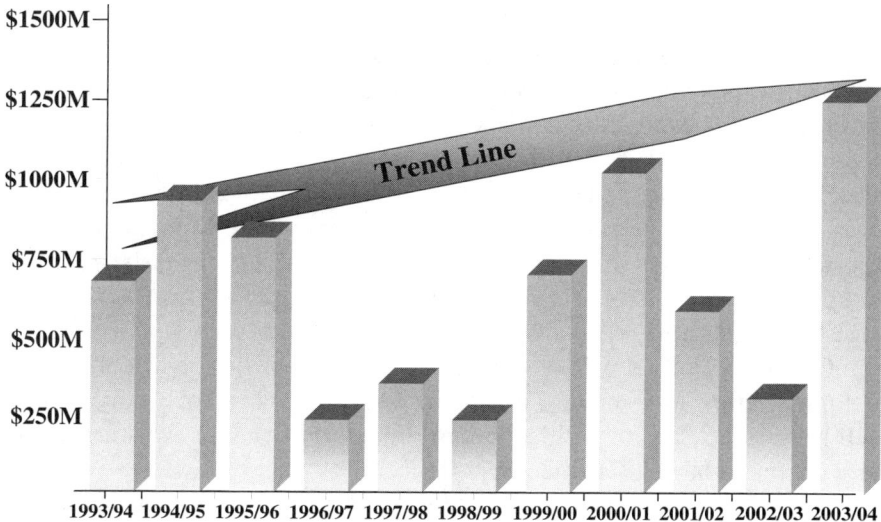

Source: Main Estimates 1992-2003. Full Cost Dollars.

current operations, a prudent government would activate appropriate replacement programmes to ensure that future contingencies can be met.

The sudden and unplanned commitment to the International Security Assistance Force (ISAF) in Afghanistan is a telling example of this problem. The projected Main Estimates for 2003/04 do not include funds for this commitment. In January 2003, prior to the ISAF commitment, the total shortfall in O&M funding to sustain the entire CF was projected to be $1,286 million for fiscal year 2003/04. The final cost of sending 3,800 personnel to Kabul is not yet known, but when the projected cost ($600-900 million) is added to the known O&M shortfall, the total shortfalls in all operation accounts for the Canadian Forces in 2003/04 would be approximately $2 billion.

As the ISAF cost was not forecasted in the O&M business plans, it is not clear how this operation will be funded. Although some money has been allocated by government to cover some costs, DND will be required to absorb future costs; and funds for this commitment can be found only by turning to the capital account and by deferring now lower-priority projects.[8]

What is more important to note is that this operation, like all other *real* operations, cannot be controlled in the way training and managerial project can be because the demands of the operation are largely unknown from day to day. All cost estimates are contingent on events that arise in the field, and at any time they may increase dramatically. Governments cannot walk away from such undertakings; nor can they demand that soldiers "do more with less" or raid the capital account endlessly – for the simple reason that this account is finite. The total dollar-cost of the mission to Kabul, along with all the other ongoing international missions of the Canadian Forces, will not likely be known until many months after the units return to Canada. The next government, therefore, may find itself trapped in "a money-pit" of commitments demanding ever-increasing and uncontrollable financial support.

The essence of Canada's crises in national defence and foreign policy is that elements of capabilities and entire capabilities are being consumed more rapidly than they can be replaced. The nature of this problem is hidden from public view by efforts to keep the present force functioning, but a close examination of activity costs as reflected in the O&M budget reveals plainly the seriousness of these approaching crises. Attempting to do more with less demoralizes and unfairly penalizes those Canadians who are on the front line. Borrowing from the future force to provide for the present force is simply a strategy that will accelerate the disintegration of both parts of the armed forces.

THE TRAINING CRISIS

The cost of training an individual from enrolment in the Canadian Forces through to the end of basic and trades-qualification training is a major factor in forecasting the capacity of the Canadian Forces to conduct operations.

For a number of reasons, but primarily because it was easier to downsize than to sustain a fixed personnel strength, the Canadian Forces overshot the Regular Force personnel reduction goal (60,000) in the years

1999-2001.[9] This problem was created by an honest, but desperate, attempt to find money in the personnel budget to transfer to the collapsing capital budget. When the defence minister reversed the policy, officials were compelled to more than double the planned annual recruiting intake to rebuild and stabilize the personnel strength at 60,000 once again.[10] (See Table 4.3.) However, the intake plan failed to address the consequences of this policy reversal in terms of training and cost and the effect it would have on the "individual training system". Rather than solving the capital imbalance in the budget, the on-again-off-again process worsened the overall circumstances of defence expenditures.

Table 4.3
Regular Force Enrollment (Intake), 1998-2004

Fiscal Year	Regular Force Intake	Remarks
1998-1999	2,600 persons	Actual
1999-2000	2,918	Actual
2000-2001	3,220	Actual
2001-2002	5,404	Actual
2002-2003	6,100	Estimate
2003-2004	5,400	Planned

The Canadian Forces follow a career-development programme based on qualification and rank. For the purposes of this study, only the first "Development Period" (DP1) is discussed. DP1 normally includes basic recruit-training, special-to-classification operational and technical training, and some advanced-classification training. To illustrate, a soldier who joins the armour branch completes Basic Recruit Training at Saint.Jean, QC, then proceeds to the Armour School in Gagetown, NB, for Qualification Level 3 (QL3) Crewman and Armour Reconnaissance Tactics training. After some time at an armour unit, the newly minted crewman may undergo QL4 Crewman training, either at the unit or at a formation "Battle School". Upon completion of this training, the crewman is eligible for Development Period 2 (DP2) training, which includes army junior-leadership courses. The total DP1 training time for a crewman is 180 days. Many classifications require more time, but no recruits can be deemed qualified and ready for deployments with a unit until they have successfully completed DP1 training.

The cost of individual training for the entire Canadian Forces was determined for this analysis by using individual-training criteria for all classifications and cost data from a 1997-2000 DND study.[11] The DP1 cost for the entire Canadian Forces, at a time when Regular Force annual intake was averaging 2,600 recruits a year, was $1,028 million per year (±10 percent). Regular Force recruit intake has doubled since 2001, but the DP1 individual training system has not received a doubling of resources. This means that money was not available to provide for training needs, and because the money is not available to purchase training equipment and to increase training staffs, DP1 candidate training is taking twice the normal time to complete. This extra time and these extra recruits significantly increase O&M costs. It is, arguably, the failure to increase funding (by approximately $1,000 million) to support the individual training system that is one of the major contributing factors to the perennial O&M funding shortfall ($1,286 million in 2003/04).

The latest production figures reveal that in May 2003, 7,872 personnel were awaiting or receiving training.[12] Given that the recruiters are annually pumping 5,000-6,000 candidates into an individual training system that was downsized in the 1990s to handle fewer than 3,000 trainees a year, one should not be surprised to discover that thousands of paid but unqualified, and therefore unusable, people are waiting to begin or to complete DP1 training.

Table 4.4 shows that the CF has many new and inexperienced service members who are in need of training and development. Sadly, there is a shortage of experienced junior leaders to carry out this task. In the army, the individual-training problem is made worse by the demands of ISAF. The army can afford to maintain only a small cadre of instructors at its schools. When the demand for training courses exceeds the cadre's capacity, additional instructors are borrowed from operational units.

The current surge in DP1 training, along with the concomitant demands of the policy to restore the militia, has forced the Combat Training Centre to bring in additional instructors from April to October of every year since 2000.[13] However, the resources of two Regular Force brigades are required to sustain the Canadian ISAF contingent in Kabul for 18 months, and the third brigade is needed to sustain other operations over the same 18-month period.[14] There are, therefore, precious few leaders who can be released from operational units and sent to the schools as instructors without impairing these units in the field.

The army staff estimates that the individual training system will meet barely half of the training demand for 2003 and 2004. Thus, the system will not be generating sufficient numbers of soldiers and leaders over the next few years to meet current and anticipated demands. This training shortfall will seriously limit military capabilities, thereby restricting the government's ability to undertake future operations in any but desperate circumstances.

The limitations of the individual training system imposed by past policy choices, and ongoing operations, have put the Canadian Forces, specifically the army, into a downward cycle that is reducing simultaneously both the quantity and the quality of personnel. "Force generation" – that is, provision of training personnel and units – must be completed before operations can be conducted. But the structure and the capacity of the individual training system must be put right before the problem of force generation can be overcome. Even if the resources to meet this objective were to be made available immediately (calculated at some $1,000 million per year for training) and a start were to be made in 2004, the system would not be in balance until some time in 2010.[15]

In summary, the individual training system is inadequate for the times. The culture of "operations first" is competing with the force-generation institutions and the policy demands. In other words, defence policy and management are contradictory. The demands of force generation are manifested in annual business-plan shortfalls (currently $1,286 million), and they contribute to high attrition rates in Basic Engagements. (In some classifications, service members never become qualified during their three-year engagement.) High attrition in turn drives the demand for even more recruits. This puts further stress on the already inadequate training system, thus exaggerating the system shortfall while decreasing the number of qualified persons entering Canadian Forces units.

The army is in some respects the "canary in the Canadian Forces coal mine". Given that its training system can meet only 50 percent of current demand and that the army is experiencing such high attrition rates in its operational and technical classifications, it is estimated that the army will fill only 75 percent of its authorized manning levels in 18 months and only 50 percent of them in 36 months.[16] To put it another way, by 2005/06, after the requisite ISAF "post-operational respites", the army will be able to field only six manoeuvre units for operations, rather than the current twelve manoeuvre units. Furthermore, since the current twelve are at only 85 percent strength, the total manoeuvre-unit capacity may well be below 50 percent by 2006/07. National defence and foreign policies cannot be met with twelve partially populated operational land units.

THE SUPPORT CRISIS

"Support" as defined by military doctrine is a term that encompasses all activities required to sustain an operational force at sea, in the air, or in the field. For the purposes of this analysis, support will be limited to acquisition, support of equipment, and infrastructure issues.

Support of a modern Canadian Forces that is geographically deployed from Esquimalt to Kabul requires sufficient spare parts, transport, medical personnel and supplies, and knowledgeable technicians to service every piece of equipment in the Canadian Forces inventory. Without adequate support, even the best combat soldiers cannot turn declarations and intentions into successful, measurable outcomes. Unfortunately, all of these categories of support, and others, are critically short. The problem is increasing with each operational deployment and is exacerbated by questionable defence-management practices, personnel attrition in important classifications, and aging equipment.

Examples of current support problems caused by past defence-management decisions are not difficult to find. During the 1980s, the Canadian Forces acquired most of its transport vehicles through regional-development initiatives. For instance, the Iltis 4X4 jeep-type vehicle, designed by Audi and VW of Germany and Belgium, was made under licence in Québec by Bombardier. The Light Support Vehicle Wheeled (LSVW), a 1.5-tonne 4X4 cargo truck designed by Iveco, a subsidiary of Fiat, was made in Kelowna by Western Star. The Medium Logistics Vehicle Wheeled (MLVW), a modified US Army M35/M36, was made by Bombardier, and the Heavy Logistics Vehicle Wheeled (HLVW), designed by Steyr of Austria, was made in Kingston by UTDC.

The Department of National Defence paid an exorbitant premium for these regionally manufactured trucks, a premium estimated at 250 percent of the original manufacturers' retail price.[17] In other words, the DND should have obtained twice the number of vehicles for the same price, or paid half as much for what it got. Buying approximately 10,000 trucks at twice the manufacturers' retail prices restricted the capital funds available for other requirements. But its consequence was only the start of the negative effects of this costly venture.

With the closure of Bombardier's vehicle production, DND had no recourse but to return to the original manufacturer for spare parts. Owning a limited-production, foreign-designed truck is very expensive. The costs of spare parts are not readily available for comparison purposes, but the DND *Cost Factors Manual* records that an Iltis jeep costs over $2.00/kilometer to operate. A similar North American jeep costs about $0.35/kilometer to operate, and the Iveco 1.5 tonne 4X4 costs about $2.50/kilometer. The HLVW is the most expensive: depending on the variant, its cost per kilometer ranges from $5 to $15.

The recent purchase of combat radios and other communication systems (The TCCCS project) provides a similar example. The army paid $1.3 billion for what can be termed a modest communication capability. Annual support costs for this equipment are over $50 million. This trend of acquiring expensive "orphan fleets" is not restricted to the army.[18] The navy's frigate programme was also subjected to regional-development strategies imposed on DND by Cabinet. It carries the same hallmarks of the capital premium and "orphan fleet" support costs.[19]

To date, attempts by DND officials to control these types of imposed and costly national acquisition practices have proven futile because they originate outside the Department's authority. The Department and defence policy and operations generally are directly challenged by these types of decision which, among other things, forces the Canadian Forces to find ways to maintain old, foreign-designed equipment of questionable operational value. But when the government orders the Chief of the Defence Staff to prepare and activate operations, he has little choice but to make do with the equipment that is at hand.

Putting regional development ahead of military efficiency and effectiveness has saddled the Canadian Forces with equipment that is very expensive to maintain. This fact has forced DND officials to rob the capital account to find funds for cost-overruns in the O&M budget. The priority for spare parts goes to equipment deployed on current operations. The inventory of spare parts for equipment not on operations is not well funded because it is considered low-priority. In some cases, the purchase of spare parts is deferred entirely while officials wait for a better budget year. This practice has been *de rigueur* since 1997. Given that 2003-2004 ongoing operational activities have already demonstrated a huge appetite for spares, Canadian-based equipment that is essential to support collective and individual training will continue to deteriorate. Again, force generation suffers. Accordingly, we can anticipate the cancellation of Primary Reserve training, which will lead to higher Primary Reserve attrition rates simply because it is impossible to train and retain young people when there is little for them to do.

The DND *Capability Outlook 2002-2012* report contains the following, extremely revealing, statement about infrastructure support:

> Sustainment success is contingent in part on the maintenance of appropriate Realty Assets (RAs) (i.e. offices, warehouses, hangars, workshops, medical centres, military jails, etc.). Under-investment in infrastructure replacement is leading to significant problems. Fully 58 percent of CF buildings are over 40 years old – most are past their original service life – and 81 percent were constructed or acquired in response to vastly differing security eras (i.e. Cold War, Korean War, WWII, and WWI). The net result is a deficiency/rust-out backlog estimated at $800M [FY 2001/2002]. Further, while 75 percent of CF RAs are currently rated as average, many buildings and workshops will decline to below-average status over the next decade. In Capability Based Planning terms, the bulk of CF RAs are poised to change from Yellow to Red in the midterm unless remedial measures are initiated. The latter will call for an unprecedented increase in Maintenance and Repair (M&R), replacement requirements and their associated funds. Base Commanders have also voiced health and safety concerns with respect to occupied buildings. If the status quo prevails it is conservatively estimated that the M&R replacement gap will grow to $2.2B in 5 years and $3.6B in 10 years.

A SUMMARY OF THE CRISIS FACTS

Before examining specific "at risk" capabilities, it is useful to emphasize the following facts:

- Finding an adequate share of the defence budget to provide funds to support capital investment to maintain military capabilities for the future force is a longstanding policy difficulty in DND. But today, after more than ten years of under-investment, and as operations increase and equipment is consumed at unplanned-for rates, the problem has become a crisis beyond the capability of DND to manage, let alone solve.
- Over the last decades, as a consequence of political decisions to award contracts for the acquisition of capital equipment as part of regional-development processes, contract costs have increased substantially.
- During the 1990s, the Canadian Forces attempted to find money for the capital account by reducing personnel strengths. This policy led to an immediate release of specially trained and hard-to-replace people, who were subsequently in great demand as operations increased unexpectedly. Moreover, when this policy was reversed by the minister of national defence – leading to a rush to recruit replacements but with no increase in the defence budget for this purpose – the training system was immediately overburdened, as was the O&M budget. The costs associated with training replacements in some categories of expertise are now beyond the capability of DND to manage or solve. As a consequence, a number of military capabilities or essential elements of them are at risk, and many will not be sustainable in the future.
- The support crisis has come into sharper focus with the increased commitment of the Canadian Forces to international stability operations. Even though units on operations have top priority for all classes of support and for qualified people, and even though officers and officials have taken risks to meet demands, the reality is that the Canadian Forces can sustain overseas only one or two battle groups of approximately 1,000-1,200 troops, two ships, and a handful of aircraft.

CAPABILITIES AT RISK

Chronic underfunding of the capital and O&M accounts, the personnel training system, and military support generally has eroded Canadian Forces capability today and placed the future force at risk.[20] The following "at risk" CF capabilities are typical of the problem (summarized in Table 4.4).

Table 4.4
Canadian Forces Capabilities at a Glance, 2003-2010[21]

Capability	State	Remarks
Strategic Command	High Risk	• Shortage of qualified personnel • Lack of electronic protocols • Lack of sufficient surveillance assets • Not network-centric • Lack of command and joint doctrine • Lack of timely intelligence • Not prepared for real-time decision-making and timely dissemination of information
Logistical Support	High Risk	• Shortage of qualified personnel • Lack of electronic interface • Inadequate support for operations • Nil operational-level surveillance • Poor fire-support coordination
Information and Intelligence	Significant Limitations; likely to go High Risk if national and international intelligence required at same time	• Shortage of qualified people • Lack of information ops doctrine • Lack of electronics and surveillance • Dysfunctional structure • HUMINT and SIGINT require investment
Strategic Mobility	High Risk	• Virtually non-existent
Conduct Operations	High Risk	• Navy virtually on a year of rest starting summer 2003. By 2004 the navy could crew 60-70% of ships. • Army at about 50% by 2004 • Air Force fleets at 30-60% availability
Force Generation	High Risk	• Individual training system inadequate • Lacking equipment, underfunded • Severe limitations prevent reaching CF Trained Effective Strength prior to 2010.

Command. Early retirements in the 1990s resulted in a shortfall of command and staff expertise in the Canadian Forces. Underfunding of training and development programmes (especially at the strategic level) has exacerbated this problem by placing inordinate burdens on those officers who remain in command, especially those in expert staff positions.

Logistical Support. In the past, the Canadian Armed Forces were highly valued. Largely because of its operational and logistical expertise and excellent military support capabilities, international organizations usually looked to Canada to provide major or leading elements of multinational operations. Today, although the individual and unit expertise remains (albeit at much reduced numbers), the logistical backbone of the Canadian Forces is crippled. Attempts to carry out demanding missions in Zaire and in other regions in the 1990s were exceedingly difficult and expensive, often requiring officers to construct ad hoc command and support arrangements and DND to hastily purchase or rent capabilities that were once common in the Canadian Forces. More worrisome is the fact that as support capabilities, including people, are used up, few replacements are either available or on the horizon to provide for future operations.

Intelligence and Information. The Canadian Forces have critical deficiencies in intelligence and command staffs. The intelligence and information crisis is likely to worsen because of two external factors: the merging of US Space Command and Strategic Command (STRATCOM) and the US Armed Forces Command's adoption of Commander-in-Chief 21st century (CINC21) command protocols.[22]

As the US Armed Forces move to their second-generation global command network, and as their space surveillance assets are moved away from NORAD (where space information was shared with the Canadian Forces), NDHQ will need to find the means (both electronic and political) to plug into our southern neighbour's intelligence and information assets if Canada hopes to maintain a viable Canadian national-surveillance system.

How much is Canada willing to pay for national surveillance? This issue, perhaps, has already been decided by the shortfall in the capital account. It is unlikely that the defence programme will be able to sustain this priority in addition to other costly projects now in train or on the horizon. Unfortunately for those officials who are trying to keep the programme in balance and on track, the effects of operations and the fast deterioration of other critical capabilities will soon outpace their work.

Strategic Mobility. Save for the Airbus aircraft that transport Canadian Forces personnel but no major equipment, the Canadian Forces have no strategic mobility of any kind. The CC-130 Hercules aircraft fleet, reportedly the oldest fleet of its type in any air force (19 of 32 were grounded in the spring of 2003), provides low-altitude, short-duration in-theatre tactical airlift. Canada might have invested in a military seaborne-transport capability, but even during the Cold War, this project was put on the backburner. Recent operations have been supported by rental of foreign air and sea carriers, most of which have been successful, with the exception of the unfortunate GTS Katie Affair.

The lack of a modern, reliable strategic-transport fleet handicaps Canadian Forces deployments and national policy independence in an era when operations are conducted mostly in faraway places and when rapid transportation assets are a critical factor for both deployment and sustainment of forces. The Australian Defence Force deployed 2,000 soldiers and their equipment by air and sea to the Solomon Islands in a few days. By contrast, the Canadian Forces took six weeks to deploy 900 army personnel and light equipment to Kabul.[23]

Conduct Operations. The sea and air capabilities are highly dependent on equipment, technicians, and periodic maintenance. The chapters on capital and personnel (Chapters 2 and 3) document the fact that many systems and classifications are at risk and that, as a consequence, the level of future operations and thus foreign policy will also be at risk. Land-based capabilities depend largely on a ready supply of trained soldiers and junior leaders, but the decline in both the quantity and quality of personnel, caused by an inadequately supported individual training system, is worrying. The chief of the defence staff has already declared that he will be unable to provide land forces for any but very small future operations. The evidence confirms this expert assessment and suggests that the decline in land-based capabilities will continue, not just for two or three years but for most of the next decade.

Force Regeneration and Transformation. A modern military force, especially one in active operations, must be able to regenerate itself and, at the same time, transform its doctrine, strategy, unit composition, and technical capabilities to match the pace of change in military, national, and international affairs. To be effective, this process must be continuous and allow for few lapses in capabilities while transformation is under way. To do otherwise is to risk the nation's safety and its independence of decision in matters of defence and foreign policy.

Regeneration and transformation are expensive and time-consuming. Leaders in the Canadian Forces understand the necessity for both processes, but they also realize that they do not have the necessary funds to do more than explore the edges of the world that the Canadian Forces is entering in 2003. Without a significant improvement in the health of the defence capital account, sustained over many years, this renewal process cannot be undertaken. Consequently, Canada will be less evident in international military operations in the future and more dependent on other nations for primary military capabilities; even the surveillance and defence of Canadian territory will be limited.

The Canadian Armed Forces have suffered a number of successive decades of reductions in defence expenditure, which have reduced some of Canada's military capabilities and eliminated others entirely. The 1987 White Paper, *Challenge and Commitment,* warned of the approaching rustout of the armed forces. *1994 White Paper on Defence* accepted this situation on the assumption that the demand for armed forces would decline after the Cold War.

The government, therefore, radically reduced the size of the Canadian Forces and effectively froze the defence budget. The demand for armed forces, however, increased, and the few funds available for force-renewal were carried into other parts of the defence programme. The Canadian Forces then entered a decade of downward-spiralling retrenchment, during which the stock of operational goods aged and was reduced by use or elimination. This aging fleet, much of it equipment acquired in the 1970s and 1980s, is very expensive to maintain, and O&M costs are consuming much of the anticipated savings of the smaller Canadian Forces.

Officers and officials in the Canadian Forces and DND have continuously juggled demands for armed forces while living on a fixed budget predicated on assumptions made in 1994. They are "managing risk", to use the current jargon, mainly by using funds intended for building the future to maintain the present force, but their ability to hold off the consequences of this strategy is reaching an end. The present force is tired and worn, and the future force will be a mere image of what Canada's defence policy and prudent political leadership will demand.

The crisis is not simply a problem for military leaders and a few officials and does not lie in the disappearance of vital military capabilities; the crisis is not only about a hamstrung foreign policy. The real crisis lies in the fact that no matter what route the government might take to put right the basic military problem, it is unlikely that any will lead to success within the next five to ten years. Managing future foreign policy and responding to domestic and international security demands without a modern, robust armed force: that is the true crisis facing Canada in 2003.

NOTES

[1] As quoted in "Armed Forces have earned rest: McCallum" by David Pugliese, *National Post*, 2 July 2003, A4.

[2] Douglas L. Bland, *Canada's National Defence*, Volume 1 *Defence Policy*, (Kingston: School of Policy Studies, Queen's University, 1997).

[3] Ibid., 183–85.

[4] Department of National Defence, Assistant Deputy Minister Public Affairs, "Roundtable," 4 June 2003.

[5] David Pugliese, "Army Wins Battle for Cash, New Equipment," *The Ottawa Citizen*, 24 July 2003, A5.

[6] Department of National Defence, *Army Transformation Plan*, dated 26 June 2003, signed by Chief of Land Staff.

[7] Conference of Defence Associations, *A Nation at Risk*, October 2002; http://www.cda-cdai.ca

[8] Department of National Defence, *Report on Plans and Priorities 2002-2003,* Annex B, Cost of Operations.

[9] Annual Report of the Chief of the Defence Staff 1999-2000, Annex D, Summary by Rank – Regular Force Personnel.

[10] Annual Reports of the Chief of the Defence Staff 2000-2001, and 2001-2002, Annex D, Summary of Recruit Intake.

[11] Major S. Curry, and Major J. Tardivel, *Canadian Forces Terms of Service Study Phase 3B: An Exercise to Cost the Investment in MOC/Career Individual Training,* 15 August 2000.

[12] Directorate of Military Human Resource Requirements (DMHRR), Monthly Report, May 2003 (referred to as LCol Smith.xls)

¹³Interview of CLS Business Planning staff, May 2003; based on CTC Co-ord Cell and CLS Task Co-ord data. The Canadian Forces Tasking Program, managed by DCDS, tracks movements of all tasked individuals.

¹⁴Army Training and Operations Framework 2003, managed by Director Army Training (Ottawa), illustrates that each OP ATHENA Roto 0 requires one brigade (2 Brigade – Petawawa); Roto 1 requires another brigade (5 Brigade Valcartier). Canada's third brigade (1 Brigade – Edmonton) is committed to sustaining the other major peace stability operations (OP PALLADIUM).

¹⁵This is based on the author's extrapolation of the data made available in Directorate of Operational Research (Corporate) report, *Assessing the Wellness of the Canadian Forces*, July 2003.

¹⁶Military Occupations Classifications briefing to Assistant Chief of Land Staff, 17 April 2003.

¹⁷For example, Iltis factory price delivered to Montreal by VW was $26,500 (1984); from Bombardier, the total unit cost was $84,500 (1984). As an officer in the Directorate of Land Requirements in the 1980s and 1990s, the author made presentations to the Office of the Auditor General of Canada on Iltis and MLVW. Those who made same for LSVW and HLVW worked on his staff.

¹⁸"Orphan fleets" is the name given by life-cycle managers to equipment that has no parent equipment.

¹⁹It is estimated that each frigate cost $600 million to produce; the same class of frigate from US Shipyards is estimated to cost US$200 million in 1985 dollars.

²⁰See Vice Chief of Defence Staff summary of CF capability gaps, entitled *Capability Outlook 2002 – 2012,* July 2002; http://www.vcds.dnd.ca/dgsp/pubs/rep-pub/CAPABILITY_OUTLOOK_E.pdf>

²¹http://www.vcds.dnd.ca/dgsp/pubs/rep-pub/intro_e.asp and http://www.oag-bvg.gc.ca/domino/other.nsf/html/00nd_e.html

²²American Unified Command Plan, 27 April 2002, and Phillipe Lagassé, *Coming Home to Roost: Canadian Indecision on BMD and the Eclipse of Canada-US Space Cooperation, On Track,* 20 December 2002. The author of *Gathering Crisis* chapter was Land Force ISTAR Coordinator for 2001/02. LF ISTAR must operate within CF Intelligence, Surveillance and Reconnaissance protocols, which must operate within CINC 21 protocols, should Canada wish to be interoperable with US forces or run a coalition headquarters.

²³Australian Defence Force News Release, "2 Royal Australian Rifles arrives in Solomon Islands, 13 C-130 flights and one ship bring in most of 2000 person peace force within one day," 25 July 2003.

CHAPTER FIVE

A Summary of Major Findings

We treat the military very well. They are very well equipped.
Prime Minister Jean Chrétien
Kabul, October 2003

Military capability, a system of systems, is the product of effective equipment, trained personnel, appropriate doctrine, command and communications systems, and logistical support which, when used in unison, enable the commanders to accomplish missions. The capability of the Canadian Armed Forces to meet government defence objectives has been eroding, is eroding, and will continue to erode; it cannot be sustained under present policies (Table 5.1). In some core capabilities, all of the major components are failing together while others are hamstrung by particular deficiencies. Two essential components are specifically endangered today: there are simply not enough trained people, or the facilities and resources to train them, to ensure that the Canadian Forces will be operationally fit in the future. Second, major equipments are failing from age and use, and the plans to replace them are inadequate to the demand.

This short summary deals primarily with the deficiencies in the capital-account portion of the defence budget and particularly with the shortfall in capital funds meant to be allocated to the acquisition of modern equipment. It is, as this study has attempted to explain, critically important to understand that core military capabilities are composed of systems within a system and that no credible capability exists if any part is defective or deficient. Nevertheless, this summary addresses mainly the equipment limitations that exist today or that will occur as older stocks disappear and are not replaced in a timely fashion. It is self-evident that without modern equipment, training cannot occur, command and support systems are unnecessary, people cannot be employed, and commanders cannot accomplish their missions.

Table 5.1
Canadian Forces Projected Activity and Capability Trends to 2007/08

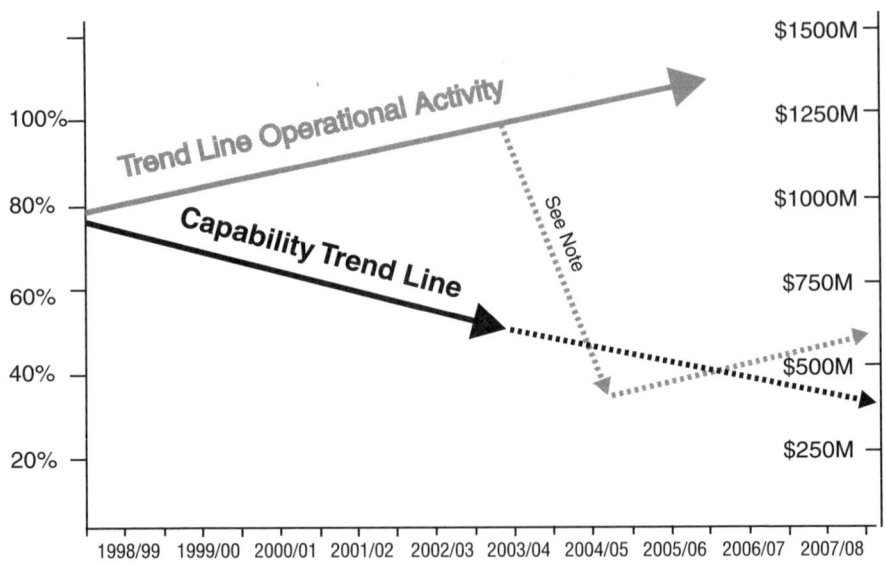

Note: Dotted line indicates DND's assumed reduction and later recovery of operational activities, beginning 2004/05.
Source: Main Estimates 1992-2003. Full Cost Dollars.

The capabilities of the Canadian Forces have been declining for about four decades. In 1985-1987, the Canadian defence budget accounted for 2.2 percent of Canadian Gross Domestic Product (GDP). Since 1994, the defence budget has dropped from about 1.7 percent to 1.1 percent: altogether, a 50 percent drop since the mid-1980s. This policy was exacerbated by the fact that the real purchasing power of the defence budget fell 50 percent faster – and farther – than did the cuts in personnel strengths, infrastructure, and operational commitments among other things. As a result costs increased even as effectiveness decreased.

In the aftermath of Budget 2003 (February 2003), the total annual indebtedness of all Canadian Forces "business plans" (the official demand for funds from elements of the Department of National Defence and the

Canadian Forces) for fiscal year 2003/2004 was $1.25 billion. By this measure, the extant structures and activities of the Canadian Forces are unsustainable.

According to National Defence Estimates, 2003/2004, the total forecast cost of all peace and stability operations, *excluding* International Security Assistance Force (ISAF Kabul), is $1.25 billion. The cost for ISAF for fiscal year 2003/2004 is estimated at $600 million, and this operation (the full cost of which will not be known until the mission is completed), when added to the unreported full cost of peace and stability operations for the Canadian Forces in 2003/2004, could reach $2 billion. It is not clear how this $2 billion cost will be funded.

THE EQUIPMENT SITUATION, 2003

Many of the Canadian Forces major platforms are at or close to the end of their effectiveness. As a consequence, Canada's military equipment is facing massive obsolescence beginning around 2005.

Defence policy is notionally aimed at allocating 23-27 percent of the defence budget to capital acquisition to maintain viable, military core capabilities. This target has not been met over the last three decades; the reality is that the allocation to the capital account has varied from 7-18 percent as a residue of other expenditures. There is, therefore, a huge capital debt or "bow wave" of unfulfilled and deferred projects pushing ahead of an ever-shrinking supply of money. Defence planners in 2003 could find only about 7 percent (or less than $1 billion) in the defence budget to allocate to the acquisition of new equipment.

Over the next 15 years, 2003-2018, the Canadian Forces needs close to $50 billion to replace obsolete fleets and to acquire new equipment if it is to sustain and restore core capabilities. Given that the projected availability of capital funds over this period is only some $20 billion, the Canadian Forces, under current policies, faces an insurmountable $30 billion shortfall for capital acquisition; that is, a shortfall of $2 billion a year for the next fifteen years.

2003-2008

The total capital demand for 2003-2008 is $23.8 billion. The actual capital funding availability for this period is $8 billion, leaving a recapitalization shortfall of some $15 billion, or $3 billion per year over the next five years.

Over the next five years, seven major platforms – the Hercules CC-130, the Medium Logistics Vehicle Wheeled (MLVW), the Main Battle Tank (MBT), the M-109 howitzer, and the Maritime Helicopter – will have reached (or be close to) obsolescence.

Extending the "life-cycle" of any of these systems beyond 2008, even if it were possible, is plainly too expensive to contemplate because this policy would put significant stress on other parts of the defence budget and would certainly detract from or sideline other operational priorities. It would only delay decisions that will have to be faced sometime and, in fact, ought to be taken now.

It is possible that two other critical elements of the core maritime capability, the four IROQUOIS class destroyers and the two Auxiliary Oiler Replenishment vessels (AOR's), both classes of vessel commissioned in the 1970s, could be life-extended through this period. However, careful cost/benefit analysis would likely argue against this option.

The Canadian Forces urgently requires four new capabilities, most of them related to the command and control of forces in operations and/or operations with allied forces. These systems include Canadian Forces Intelligence, Surveillance and Reconnaissance (CFISR), Polar Star, National Military Space Capability, and the army Intelligence Surveillance Target Acquisition and Reconnaissance project (ISTAR); funding for these projects over the longer term is not assured.

Impact Statement. Most of these capabilities cannot be recouped during 2003-2008 even if the government were to attempt to do so immediately. Consequently, over this period, the Canadian Forces could lose most of its logistics sea-lift, air-lift, and land-lift capabilities. At the end of this period, the Canadian Forces air-lift capability would be reduced to 13 of the newer CC-130s (vintage, 1970s) and 5 Airbus CC-150s (which cannot carry large equipment) to support its world-wide and domestic operations.

The federal government's acquisition practices, and the unavailability of aircraft and operational support ships, suggest that the Canadian Forces will not be able to restore its operational transport capability until 2013, at the earliest. The likelihood of up to ten years without operational transport capabilities severely limits participation in international peace and stability operations throughout this decade and the next.

If the destroyers or the AORS cannot be maintained, any international deployment of a Canadian naval task group – a major capability called for in *1994 Defence White Paper* – would be problematic without foreign assistance.

2008-2013

Over the period 2008-2013, an additional $10 billion will be required for capital acquisition.

Two major fleets, the Heavy Logistics Vehicle Wheeled (HLVW) and the Light Support Vehicle Wheeled (LSVW), will reach the end of their effective lives in this period. Three platforms – the CC-150 transport, the Tactical Helicopters, and the Submarines – reach their mid-life refit/life-extension point. Because capital funding will not be sufficient to recover from the capital shortfall of the 2003-2008 period, the government might be forced to choose between correcting the shortfall in either logistics transportation or maritime capabilities. It will be impossible to do both with the funds projected for the period.

By the end of the second five-year window (2013), the air force might endure the greatest loss of capabilities and be reduced to a small transportation fleet, a tactical aviation fleet, and a much-reduced CF-18 inventory.

2013-2018

The 2013-2018 period demands a massive re-capitalization that is projected to exceed $25 billion. During this period, if funding is not provided soon, the most critical decision to be made is whether Canada will maintain a core land-force capability or a core maritime capability. The projected funds for this period simply will not sustain both capabilities at credible operational levels.

CONCLUSIONS

The requirement for capital renewal vastly exceeds the amount of capital monies available to the defence establishment over the next 15 years.

In effect, current capital allocations are adequate for about one and a half core capabilities *if the capital funding status quo can be maintained.* If this portion of the defence budget continues to fall and if funding for capital acquisition is not increased, then the air force will likely disappear through the 2008-2013 time-frame, and either the army or navy will disappear in the same time-frame.

To avert this danger, the Canadian Armed Forces need a controlled and dedicated capital infusion of more than $2 billion/year for each of the next 15 years to provide the estimated $50 billion that will be needed to address capital replacements and the transformation of the armed forces. And this increase is, of course, over and above personnel and O&M costs, which can be expected to increase in real terms throughout the period.

By most estimates, if Canada is to sustain the current Canadian Forces set of core capabilities for national command, support, maritime, land, and air force operations while maintaining a Reserve element, then the defence portfolio will require an annual defence allocation of $18.5 billion (or 1.6 percent of GDP) – an annual increase of $5 billion in defence expenditures, beginning in 2004.

In *1994 Defence White Paper,* the government warned Canadians that, "were Canada to abandon the capability to participate effectively in the defence of North America, NATO-Europe and victims of aggression elsewhere, we would stand to lose a significant degree of respect and influence abroad."[1] The real cost to Canadians if this $18.5 billion allocation is not provided, however, will be not simply a loss of international respect, but most likely the loss of control over most of Canada's territory and, ultimately, the forfeiting of national sovereignty. Canadians, it would appear, had best prepare themselves for these ominous apprehensions.

NOTE

[1] Canada, DND, *1994 Defence White Paper*, Ottawa, 1994, p. 12.

CHAPTER SIX

An Alternative Future

> Many nations had an appetite for power without teeth, but Canada [during the Cold War] had developed both the appetite and the teeth for a new international role.
>
> *Paul Martin Sr.*
> *Minister for External Affairs, 1964*

Political futures are rarely inevitable. Policy is not self-enforcing. Therefore, outcomes – actual policy – can be manipulated by decisions and choices. Nevertheless, both politics and policy are subject to "the tyranny of past decisions", and as future governments attempt to formulate national security and defence policies, they may find that many doors have been closed by decisions taken by previous cabinets.

Prime ministers, of course, will not necessarily be impotent, and could take steps to reorder the fundamentals of defence policy. They will not, however, be able to reverse past decisions easily or quickly. Thus, as prime ministers work to overcome the legacy of the past decade, they will have to address, day by day, the unavoidable crisis brought on by the inadequacies of the present Canadian Armed Forces.

The worsening state of Canada's military capabilities and governments' failures over a long period to invest adequately in people, military institutions, modern technologies – in the wide range of paraphernalia required to generate military capabilities – is the root cause of the gathering crisis, but not the crisis itself. Foreign policy, insofar as it must be backed by credible military capabilities, is likely to fail as the decay of military capabilities accelerates. Relations between Canada and the United States, the primary concern of Canadian foreign policy and most prime ministers, could continue to suffer as the Canadian Forces becomes less capable. But these effects are not the central crisis, either. Two factors represent the crisis in full array: Prime Minister Martin's inability to remedy the military crisis and its effects on foreign policy during the tenure of the next government, and the difficulty of finding some way to defend Canadians and their interests and to uphold Canada's international responsibilities.

Which doors are closed? What could future prime ministers do to avoid this gathering national crisis? Governments could stop sending all but token forces overseas, but this would only confirm Canada's impotence. Governments might cut some military capabilities to bolster others. However, past policies have nearly eliminated any reserve, and a new round would cut into sparse "core capabilities." One fact is plain: the looming foreign-policy crisis produced by the lack of military capabilities cannot be solved by cutting the few capabilities that remain. Canada, some suggest, could select "niche roles" for the armed forces and reinforce these. But too often the things such advocates usually want to do are not things the world wants done. What, then, should the Canadian Forces be prepared to do? Prudence and experience suggest that the Canadian Forces will be ordered to do over the next ten years the same types of things that it has done in the past ten years – providing small and medium-sized land, sea, and air combat units to use coercive means to help stabilize unruly parts of the world.

Governments might try to spend their way out of the crisis. In the early 1950s, it took several years to satisfy the Cold War demand for building from a small base a credible force of some 120,000 people equipped with modern arms, even though the government committed vast resources to this mobilization and increased the defence budget by 135 percent in just a few years. Overcoming today's problem could take a comparative effort, but even that would not resolve the immediate foreign-policy crisis.

Time, not money, is the master of this situation. It takes time – in many cases, years – to change policy goals into military fact: to train leaders, build ships, acquire equipment, and then fashion operational capabilities from the separate pieces. Thus, future prime ministers will have to live with a diminished role in international security affairs, and diplomats will have to manage the consequences.

Constructing future policy on the foundations of the present policy will weaken Canada's national security and defence and disable foreign policy in many important respects. This end will arrive sooner rather than later if the sinking capability trend is allowed to continue, and it will be increasingly expensive, time-consuming, and difficult to overturn as each month passes. This, then, is the predicted future – national security, defence, and foreign policies essentially disarmed by Canada's choice, with only faint hope of timely rescue.

WHAT MIGHT BE DONE TO ALTER THIS PREDICTED FUTURE?

An alternative future ought to provide military capabilities adequately structured to meet the current foreseeable objectives with respect to defence, foreign policy, and domestic security. A future policy must provide for the present force and acknowledge the need for sufficient flexibility – mostly in terms of funding – to meet the volatile circumstances of the world-order era. It must concurrently, but separately, address the needs of the future force by confirming and supporting a predictable capital programme well into the future if governments are to avoid the type of cyclical disarmament that has characterized Canadian defence policy over many decades. The most important and distinctive feature in an alternative future must be the dedication of Canada's political elite to the vigorous and vigilant oversight of national security and defence as the first responsibilities of government.

A blueprint for such an alternative future might include the following elements.

"A Vigilant Parliament". Canadians alone are responsible for Canada's national defence, and that responsibility is the dominant obligation of Parliament. These two ideas are traditional rhetoric in the Canadian political community, in government policy papers, and in public discord, but rarely do they guide policy in fact. As the 1994 Special Joint Committee of the Senate and the House of Commons, reported to Parliament, "the members of the Special Joint Committee shared from the beginning [of their review] one important conviction – that Canada's defence policy is not simply a matter for the minister or for the thousands of dedicated men and women of the Canadian Forces. It requires the attention of Parliament and the Canadian people."[1] Ironically, the *Inquiry Into the Deployment of the Canadian Forces to Somalia* reached much the same conclusion, but on evidence that Parliament had not heeded well enough the warning of its own Special Joint Committee. The Commissioners,

therefore, warned Parliament again: "Civil control of the military may be a defining characteristic of liberal democracies, but it does not occur invariably. Civil control of the military in Canada and abroad should come from attentive citizens acting through an informed, concerned and vigilant Parliament."[2]

Parliament more recently has become more attentive, as the convening of a Senate committee on national security and defence attests, but this increased attention by itself has not prompted a comprehensive review of national security or defence policy. As the government begins the next round of policy reviews, a major theme within that process ought to be how "a vigilant Parliament" could more effectively oversee security and defence policy, defence management, and operations. The quest is not simply for a passive observer, but for senators and members of parliament to become full and inquisitive partners in decisions aimed at ensuring that Canada is adequately and properly defended.

Consensus Building. Federal government ministers, and principally the prime minister in this policy area, have absolute control over defence policy and the direction and control of the Canadian Armed Forces. If they are wise, however, they will acknowledge the expertise of professional officers and the advice offered to them by the chief of the defence staff. Government ministers, moreover, must depend on the chief of the defence staff and his subordinates if they are to achieve the government's defence and military objectives. This sharing of responsibility for national defence cannot be avoided, but it need not be a cause of friction. It can, in fact, be a boon to governments trying to build and direct an effective and efficient national defence.

Governments' defence policies are most successful, and military leaders most helpful to them, when political and military leaders construct together a consensus on critical issues of defence policy. The way forward depends on the ability of the prime minister and the ministers of national defence, foreign affairs, and finance, in committee with Canada's military leaders, to reach agreement on the objectives of national defence, the range and size of military capabilities to be supported, the funds that will be allocated to the main segments of the defence budget, and the general conditions under which the armed forces will be deployed and employed.

This type of consensus is best developed through direct discussions that provide opportunities for the government to describe its defence goals to the chief of the defence staff. He and his staff can assess the objectives from a technical point of view and then offer detailed proposals to meet them. Differences and contradictions that may arise can then be addressed and resolved directly in subsequent consultations. The gathering crisis is now so serious that the prime minister must lead this consensus-building process. He must also directly oversee follow-on decisions to ensure they are consistent with the intent of the consensus and have the full support of the ministers of national defence, foreign affairs, and finance and of the chief of the defence staff.

Sustaining Core Capabilities. Canadian security, defence, and foreign policies require effective, well-armed military forces that can be deployed in domestic land, sea, and air spaces and overseas. Core capabilities are designed to meet these demands; they are themselves composed of a few critical, basic elements, including people, combat ships and aircraft, army combat units of various types, long-range air and sea transportation units, communications and surveillance assets, support resources and units, and training establishments. Although the balance between these elements and their technical composition may vary over time, it is unlikely that the Canadian Forces could meet future domestic or foreign missions without them. Today, these capabilities are not being sustained, and they must be reinvented as they age. Furthermore, there are few national industries or international agreements to sustain the capabilities on a continual basis. The alternative future would ensure that core capabilities are continuously renewed, either by national industries or through standing contracts with foreign suppliers.

Making the Sharp End Sharper. Many people, in good faith but with little practical experience, when asked how they might "fix" defence policy at no cost, often suggest ways to cut core operational capabilities – "get rid of the tanks" is a typical response. But the defence problem is a shortfall in core capabilities: How can it be solved by cutting into them?

Determining the true cost of the Canadian Forces is a challenge. The 2002/03 Main Estimates indicate that about 44 percent of the defence budget goes to those who are charged with generating sea, land, and air capabilities. From another perspective, about half of the defence budget is spent on military capability related to operations, and the remainder on various managerial activities. The authors note, for example, that even though the Canadian Forces has been reduced by 50 percent over the last 40 years, overhead (measured as the increase in supervisory groups) has increased in the same time frame by 300 percent. If a significant portion of these managerial funds could be transferred to force generation and operational accounts, then a corresponding portion of the annual $5 billion shortfall identified in this study might be found from within the current defence budget.

Rather than cutting into core military capabilities, the better alternative is to decide that, henceforth, creating and sustaining these core capabilities effectively and economically at the expense of managerial activities will be at the centre of defence policy. This goal would require a huge redistribution of the resources allocated to national defence and the Canadian Forces, and a reordering of attitudes as well. In a word, policy must be aimed at transformation, a process directed at getting the most core capability from each defence dollar. No one should assume, however, that this process might turn away the gathering crisis, because even in the best of circumstances, it might take many years before this transformation is fully effective.

Defence-Funding Reform. Canadian governments typically provide to their own defence policies whatever funds are available after other domestic needs have been addressed. In this alternative future, national defence would be allocated funding that is commensurate with the demands of policy. This objective would require careful assessments of those policy demands before policies are announced. In other words, future white papers on national defence might include two main sections: one to define defence objectives in terms of military capabilities and missions and another to provide, in detail, cost projections indicating how those objectives would be met.

An alternative future would also see defence funds "voted" in two distinct segments. The first would cover personnel and O&M costs with built-in "threshold funds" to provide for unexpected expenditures during any fiscal year resulting from, for example, unforecasted deployments and support to the provinces. Historically, defence has been able to absorb incremental costs – net of revenues – in the order of 1.25 per cent of annual defence funding. Federal central agencies should anticipate these demands and hold a special and specific defence and security fund to meet them and make arrangements to distribute them without the usual bureaucratic hassle that is common in 2003.

The second distinct segment of defence allocations should go to the capital account. The establishment of individual capital accounts for specific core capabilities would greatly assist in smoothing out annual resource demands. Under this funding mechanism, an ongoing level of investment would be allocated to the capital account. During years where funding requirements are low, funds would accumulate and then be expended during peak expenditure years. Such capital accounts would provide ongoing funding for a capability that could be drawn upon when needed.[3]

This policy idea would require an annual funding allocation to each core capability that would accumulate in that specific account to sustain it and its critical elements, as required. These specific capital accounts would be, to some extent, a reallocation of funding from other, lesser capital priorities, unless incremental funding were allocated for this purpose from the central agencies. Nevertheless, if the capabilities were established as organizational priorities, then their funding would seem assured. Specific capital accounts also provide governments with the flexibility to direct funds to enhance particular defence capabilities during periods of budgetary surplus.

The aim of this alternative policy is to ensure that the CDS and officials are not forced to raid the capital account to pay overhead. It is also aimed, not too subtly, at preventing any officer or official – and even the minister of national defence – from arbitrarily shifting funds within the general pot of defence money. Achieving this end, however, demands careful, policy-oriented auditing of the fund. The most appropriate body for this purpose is Parliament or, more specifically, a standing committee of the House of Commons. This committee would be charged with oversight of both the defence capital programme and that segment of the defence fund that is allocated to the capital account.

THE DEFENCE REVIEW 2003-2004

The fundamentals of Canada's national defence policy are not sound. Military capabilities are eroding quickly from age, use, and obsolescence, among other factors. The effect of this decay, now obvious in the Canadian Forces, will soon become as obvious in foreign policy and may have a serious negative influence on Canada's ability to protect its national sovereignty. Members of the Canadian Armed Forces are on near-continuous duty in dangerous circumstances, and in too many cases they are being asked to "do more with less." Facilities to train replacement personnel are overloaded and under stress, as are the instructors who are double-tasked to instruct new recruits.

The story of the travails of the present Canadian Forces may not be new, but what is increasingly evident is that the future force supposedly intended to replace it may be in even worse condition. The lack of follow-on equipment is serious, but as this study suggests, the disappearance of an entire cohort of younger personnel meant to provide leaders for the future is an even more serious concern. The problems of the present force can, perhaps, be managed for a few more years through emergency funding, the use of reserve forces, expensive maintenance on "clapped-out, operational junk", and the skill and dedication of members of the Canadian Forces.

The future force, however, cannot be plucked out of thin air and thinner budgets. Even if governments were to grasp the problem and provide unlimited funds, it may not be possible to save some capabilities, simply because new equipment is not immediately available. In every case, time will be needed to acquire military assets, to recruit and train new people, and to weld these two elements into usable military capabilities. In the meantime, the government will have to find ways to manage its national security, defence, and foreign policies with few credible military means.

A review of national defence policy, promised by every national political party, is clearly in the offing. If experience is a true guide, then a new review might soon take off in many directions and become scattered among numerous defence issues. This harmful habit can be averted only if the next prime minister takes control of the process himself (as Pierre

Trudeau did during the 1968-70 review) and points it in a specific direction.

The researchers and authors of this study recommend that those conducting the defence policy review, no matter from where they may be assembled, be given a very specific set of tasks. The review committee (one assumes a committee) must first illustrate for the government and the public the very serious nature of the future force crisis – expanding, perhaps, on this research with the advantages the committee will have in staff and access to classified information from government sources. Second, the committee must deliver to the government conclusions concerning the life expectancy of core capabilities and major elements within these capabilities. This section of the committee's report must include recommendations on how the government might rectify or forestall the most serious future deficiencies, at least temporarily. Finally, and crucial to the review process if it is to have any relevance at all, the committee must make recommendations to guide the government out of the deep and precipitous decline in military capabilities it is now facing.

These are very demanding and difficult assignments. If they are to be met, they require the earnest dedication of a committee of the best civilian and military talent in the country. Prime Minister Paul Martin has already announced that he will convene some form of defence-policy review in 2004 – it is an opportunity that must not be squandered. Waste, in the view of the authors of this report, could not be greater than if the committee and the process turned its sights and attention on the wrong objectives. The inadequacies of policies to sustain and continually reconstitute Canada's armed forces is the source of the gathering crisis in national security, defence, and foreign policy. If this crisis of the future force is not resolved within the next few years, then Canada will be truly disarmed, and the consequences of that fact may be too stressful for the nation to bear in an increasingly dangerous, interconnected world.

NOTES

[1] Canada, Senate of Canada, *Report of the Special Joint Committee on Canada's Defence Policy: Security in a Changing World* (Ottawa: Minister of Public Works and Government Services, 1994), 1.

²Canada, *Report of the Commission of Inquiry into the Deployment of Canadian Forces to Somalia,* Volume 5 (Ottawa: Minister of Public Works and Government Services, 1997), 1453–61.

³The United States Department of Defense established a Capital Account in 1992, named the National Defense Sealift Fund (NDSF) to increase sealift capability on a long-term basis. See the 2002 RAND Corporation report, *Options for Funding Aircraft Carriers* by J. Birkler, J. Schank, and J.Chiesa.

Historical Annex

Era	Geo-Political Context	Policy Direction	Statistics	Remarks
1930s	• Pact of Paris, 1928 • League of Nations • Economic Depression • Militant nationalism: Germany, Italy, Japan	• Canada signed the Paris Pact of 1928, which described "a war", as "an aggression", as "an international crime", and limited settlement of all disputes, of whatever nature, to "pacific means." • Canada disarmed because war had been declared illegal.	**1939 (Personnel)** Navy: 1,769 Army: 4,492 Air Force: 2,948 Totals: 9,209	• Unilateral military action by Nazi Germany and Fascist Italy and ineffectiveness of Paris Pact led to general war in Europe. • Canada was poorly prepared for WWII. Its largest contribution was light infantry, the easiest type of force to generate.
WWII 1939-1945	• Allies versus Axis powers	• Ensuring peace through collective action.	**Serving in WWII (Personnel)** Navy: 106,522 Army: 730,625 AF: 249,624 Totals: 1,086,771	• Total cost of war estimated at (1947 dollars) 20.25 billion, approx. 45% of GDP. • Deferring military intervention from 1936 to 1939 resulted in the need for a massive war effort.

1946-1947	• Allies win WWII
	• Demobilization and reintegration of service members to civilian community without creating a recession
	• Nuclear weapons
	• Berlin Airlift
	• United Nations as an institution to prevent aggression leading to general war
		Canada's Defence 1947
		• Like a White Paper (Claxton, MND)
		• Reduce defence expenditures
		• Reduce three service departments under three ministers to one – MND
		• Integration of Services headquarters
		• Reorganization of Commands
		• Three roles for armed services:
		  1. Defence of Canada
		  2. Assist civil power
		  3. Voluntary collective action with allies or under UN
			1947 (Personnel)
			Navy: 6,821
			Army: 13,985
			AF: 11,804
			Totals: 32,610
				• Most Canadians were convinced that WWII was a result of pre-war laissez-faire.
				• Most Canadian politicians were committed to taking a prominent role in international affairs.
				• 1947 defence budget $240 million, about 15% of National Budget.

Historical Annex 123

Korean War 1950-1953	• Cold War • NATO formed in 1949 • Fear of aggression in Europe and actual aggression in Korea • Conviction to support collective action under UN and NATO • Canada was economically stronger than most NATO nations.	• Continuation of Claxton policies (voluntary collective action with allies and under UN). • Army commitment to NATO is one division (a 7,000-strong brigade stationed in West Germany). Remainder in Canada. • Air Division stationed in France and Germany. • Naval and naval air forces earmarked for SACLANT.	**(Regular Force Personnel)** 1949: 41,676 1950: 47,185 1951: 68,427 1952: 95,394 1953: 104,427	• Expansion of defence capabilities to meet collective action.
1954-1963	• Fear of Cold War going hot • Nuclear weapons • Intercontinental missiles • Soviet air threat to North American continent • 1956 – Suez Crisis • 1962 – Cuban Missile Crisis	• "Difficult indeed for the Canadian government to reject any major defence proposal which the United States presents with conviction as essential for the security of North America." Dept of External Affairs, October 1953. • 1956 – Canada proposed a large-scale international force to be deployed between Israel and Egypt. • DEW line built • 1958 – NORAD • 1959 – Cancellation of Arrow aircraft. • 1959 – USA-Canada Defence Production Sharing Arrangement. • Canada acquired a nuclear capability for air-to-air missiles, bombs, and artillery.	**(Personnel)** **1954** Navy: 16,955 Army: 50,248 AF: 45,596 Total: 112,799 **1956** Total: 117,177 **1965** Total: 114,164 Defence expenditures averaged 5.7% of GDP for this period.	• The 1950s recorded Canadian defence policy becoming increasingly enmeshed with Western collective-defence efforts dominated by the U.S. • Participation in NATO and NORAD determined the type of forces. • Canada had both the appetite and teeth to discourage international aggression.

...continued

Era	Geo-Political Context	Policy Direction	Statistics	Remarks
1963-1968 (Pearson)	• American-Soviet relations slowly improved. • Western alliance governments were reducing defence expenditures. • American involvement in Vietnam. • Anti-war movements. • Growth of separatist movement in Canada. • Centennial of Confederation	• Government declared its acceptance of a nuclear role and the need for Canada to contribute to allied solidarity, but real expenditures on defence declined. • 1964 White Paper reaffirmed all existing roles of NATO and NORAD. For NATO roles the emphasis was placed on "force-in-being". Eight air squadrons and a brigade group remained in Europe, but less emphasis was placed on reinforcement. • Canadian-based units started to atrophy. • Major change was intent to integrate three services into a single headquarters by abolishing the navy, army, and air force as distinct entities.	**(Personnel)** **1968:** 98,473 full-time Regular Force personnel Expenditures on defence were 3.8% of GDP.	• From 1962 to 1968, the three services in total shrank by approx. 20,000 persons. • In February 1968, the Canadian Forces was established with three subordinate commands, MARCOM, MOBCOM, AIRCOM. • Growing pride in Canada gave rise to a need for a more independent foreign policy.
1968-1983 (Trudeau)	• Changing sentiment toward East-West relationships. • Nuclear deterrent rested with U.S. • In 1970s NATO sought to improve its conventional force posture through "flexible response". • Nixon doctrine – allies carried greater conventional force burden.	• External policy would reflect domestic priorities. • 1971 White Paper reduced forces in Germany by half, moved European forces from forward defence to reserve posture, cancelled nuclear role, and terminated reinforcement brigade to central front. • CAST brigade – reinforced Norway or Denmark. • Aircraft carrier was de-commissioned. • "the scope for useful and effective peace-keeping activities now appears more modest than it did earlier, despite the persistence of widespread violence in many parts of the world." (1971 White Paper)	**(Personnel)** **1972:** 81,626 **1976:** 77,929 Expenditures on defence were 2.2% of GDP. **1983:** 81,603	• Cutbacks in personnel seriously eroded capabilities. • 4CMBG(Europe) at one point was down to 58% of its authorized peacetime establishment. • Lack of a mobilization plan and a shortage of personnel eroded Primary Reserves. • From 1968 to 1973, defence expenditures actually shrank. In 1972/73, capital purchases were down to 8% of defence budget (a historical low). • Toward the end of his mandate, Trudeau increased defence expenditures.

Historical Annex 125

1984-1993 (Mulroney)	• U.S. regarded Cold War as an economic war. President Reagan enhanced conventional force spending. • Canada had closer relationship to U.S. • Canadian debt required $44 billion annual servicing. • Strategic Defence Intiative (Star Wars) • 1989 – End of Cold War • Early 1990s – Canadian Forces in Europe were withdrawn. • Peace sustainment operations increased. • 1991 – Gulf War • 1992-93 – Croatia, Bosnia, Somalia.	• Conservative government pledged increase in defence expenditure and commitment to collective defence. • 1986 Department of External Affairs paper stressed: – Canada's welfare depended on the international political, economic, and strategic situation. Therefore, active involvement in international affairs was a necessity. • 1987 White Paper emphasized NATO and the opportunity it afforded Canada. • Forces in Europe were augmented by 1,200 persons. • NORAD was modernized. • Major fleet replacements: Sea King maritime helicopter, Main Battle Tanks, nuclear submarines. • Traditions were restored to services.	**(Personnel)** 1984: 82,046 1989: 86,863 1993: 75,629 • Expenditures on defence were 2.1% of GDP. **(Personnel)** 1990: 8,236 military personnel were stationed in Europe. 1993: 4,754 served on "peace-keeping" operations. 1994: Canadian Forces serving in Europe were no longer recorded in Estimates.	• Faced with a large federal deficit and continuing public demand for social services, the Mulroney government was unable to increase defence spending significantly. • The inherited commitment-capability gap re-emerged. • In complete reverse to Trudeau Liberals, who cut then restored funding, the Conservatives increased then limited defence expenditures.

...continued

Era	Geo-Political Context	Policy Direction	Statistics	Remarks
1993-2004 (Chrétien)	• Reunification of East and West Germany. • Peace Dividend. • A safer world • Staggering fiscal deficit.	• An effective, realistic, and affordable policy: The 1994 White Paper • 1994 Defence Economic Review • Base closures • Regular Force set to shrink to 60,000 by 1999.	**(Personnel)** **1994:** 72,363 **2004:** 62,086 (paid full-time – estimate). 53,250 (TES) • Approx. 8,000 on basic training to make up for under-strength. • Budgets of 1994, 95, 96, 97, 98 sequentially reduced defence expenditures by 23% in 1993 dollars, or 30% in 1999 dollars. • Expenditures on defence averaged 1.1% of GDP.	Chrétien government effectively repeated the earlier Liberal government approach: cut significantly at outset, then restored funding when pressure mounted.

Notes: Although successive governments appear to cut and restore funding, the general trend as illustrated in Table A.1 is a constant reduction of defence expenditures.

Table A.1
Canadian Defence Budgets as Percentage of Gross Domestic Product (GDP)

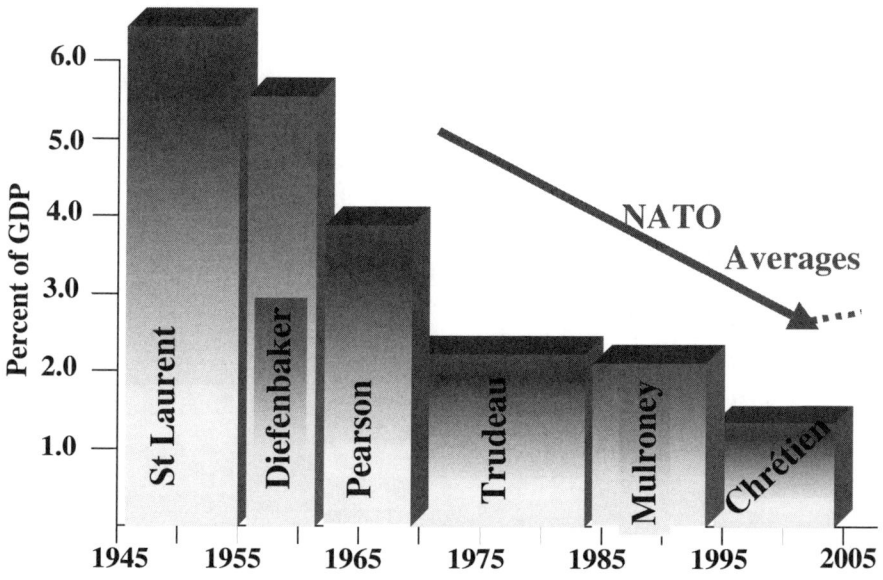

Glossary

A310	Airbus – CC-150 Polaris: a twin-engine, high-speed, commercial jet Aircraft that can be converted to any one of several main cabin arrangements for passenger and/or freight transportation.
ADATS	Air Defence Anti-Tank System: a highly mobile low-level air defence unit designed to provide air defence protection for mobile troops as well as ground installations. This self-contained weapon system is mounted on a tracked vehicle.
ADM (HR-MIL)	The Assistant Deputy Minister (Human Resources – Military) is responsible for military personnel in the Canadian Forces.
AGS	Armoured Gun Systems. The 1995 Armour Gun System is based on a track chassis. The AGS turret (105mm low profile) was installed on the Stryker 8X8 wheeled chassis and became MGS (Mobile Gun System) Stryker.
ALSC	Afloat Logistics and Sealift Capability
AMOR	Annual military occupation review
AOR	Auxiliary Oil Replenishment Vessels: an operational support ship capable of refuelling and resupplying naval ships at sea. Canada has two AORs. Can also mean Area of Responsibility
ARL	Admiralty Research Laboratory (Royal Navy). The ARL plotting table was used in the Ops Rooms of Canadian ships during WW II and up to the1970s.
ASW	Anti-Submarine Warfare
ATL	Advanced Training List
AVGP	Armoured Vehicle General Purpose: a family of six-wheeled armoured vehicles that includes the Grizzly

	Armoured Personnel Carrier, the Cougar Armoured Car, and the Husky recovery vehicle.
AVRP	Auxiliary Vessels Replacement
Bison	An eight-wheeled Armoured Personnel Carrier. Originally designed as an infantry section carrier, they are now being converted into support variants for the new Light Armoured Vehicle (LAV III).
BTL	Basic Training List
CADRE	Command and Control, and Area Air Defence Replacement
CBO	Congressional Budget Office (US)
CC-130	Hercules: a four-engine tactical transport aircraft pressed into service to provide strategic (global) airlift. The initials E, H, J designate various models and upgrade types.
CC-150	Polaris: an Airbus passenger jet modified to provide logistics support and move troops. Canada has five.
CDA	Conference of Defence Associations
CDAI	Conference of Defence Associations Institute
CDS	Chief of the Defence Staff
CF	Canadian Forces: informal term for the Canadian Armed Forces (CAF)
CF-18	Hornet: a multi-role jet aircraft capable of shooting down enemy aircraft or, when equipped with Precision Guided Munitions (PGMs) capable of attacking targets on the ground.
CFISR	Canadian Forces Intelligence Surveillance and Reconnaissance
CH-124A	Sea King (helicopter): a ship-based helicopter with both day and night flight capabilities, and is carried aboard many Canadian Maritime Command destroyers, frigates, and replenishment ships.
Chapter VII	Missions Chapter VII of the UN Charter deals with "action with respect to threats to the peace, breaches of the peace and acts of aggression" peace enforcement missions.
CINC21	Commander-in-Chief 21st Century
CO	Commanding Officer
Coyote	An eight-wheeled armoured reconnaissance vehicle equipped with a sensor system capable of night observation.

Glossary   131

	It is a highly mobile, well-armed, and well-protected reconnaissance variant of the Light Armoured Vehicle (LAV) family employed in the conduct of battlefield reconnaissance and surveillance missions at the battlegroup and brigade levels.
CRA	Compulsory Retirement Age
DELEX	Destroyer Life Extension
DEO	Direct Entry Officer
DGPA	Director General Public Affairs
DLR	Depot-Level Reparables
DMC	Defence Management Committee
DMSP	Defence Management Studies Program
DND	Department of National Defence
DP	Development Periods
ELE	Estimated Life Expectancy
F/A-18	Fighter Aircraft – US version of the CF-18 Hornet. The F/A-18 *Hornet*, an all-weather aircraft, is used as an attack aircraft as well as a fighter. In its fighter mode, the F/A-18 is used primarily as a fighter escort and for fleet air defense; in its attack mode, it is used for force projection, interdiction, and close and deep air support.
FLIR	Forward Looking Infra-red
FMTV	Family of Medium Tactical Vehicles
FRP	Force Reduction Plan
FTA	First Target Acquisition
FY	Fiscal year
GDP	Gross Domestic Product
HLVW	Heavy Logistic Vehicle Wheeled. It provides the Army with a heavy lift transport capability. Eleven different variants of this vehicle are currently serving in the Canadian Forces. The Army uses the HLVW to help support a wide variety of missions including territorial defence, domestic emergencies, combat support, and peacekeeping. It is a cross between a transport truck and an off-road vehicle.
HR	Human Resources
HSVW	Heavy Support Vehicle Wheeled

HUMINT	Human Intelligence
ICT	Information and Communications Technology
ISAF	International Security Assistance Force
ISTAR	Intelligence Surveillance Target Acquisition and Reconnaissance
IT&E	Individual Training and Education
JSF	Joint Strike Fighter
KC-135	United States Air Force airplane. The KC-135 Stratotanker's principal mission is air refuelling. It can provide aerial refuelling support to Air Force, Navy, and Marine Corps aircraft as well as aircraft of allied nations.
LAV III	Light Armoured Vehicle
LF AMOR	Land Forces (army) Annual Military Occupation Review
LIFEX	Life Extension as in Frigate Life Extension and Aurora Life Extension programmes
LRPA	Long-Range Patrol Aircraft: a four-engined aircraft capable of maritime aerial surveillance and anti-submarine warfare.
LSVW	Light Support Vehicle Wheeled, 1.5 tonne 4x4 cargo truck. The LSVW is used throughout the battlefield in such roles as command and control, troop transport, line laying, medical evacuation, maintenance, administration, and light cargo. The vehicle is air transportable in a CC-130 Hercules aircraft. It is employed in all land force missions, including territorial defence, domestic emergencies, and peacekeeping.
LTCP	Long Term Capital Plans
M-109	A self-propelled medium howitzer
M&R	Maintenance and Repair
M113A3	Refurbished and upgraded variant of the M113; a fully tracked armoured personnel carrier. The role of the new M113 variants is to provide the Army with combat support and combat service support vehicles to augment the new LAV III fleet.
M1A1	Abrams main battle tank; has a 120mm gun (US)
MA	Managing Authority
Mar Hel	Maritime Helicopter

MARS	Maritime Surface/Sub Surface: a naval officer classification
MBT	Main Battle Tank: a fully tracked armoured fighting vehicle equipped with a turret-mounted gun.
MCDV	Maritime Coastal Defence Vessel: a Canadian-designed and -built corvette.
MLVW	Medium Logistics Vehicle Wheeled: the backbone of the Army's logistic support fleet. These vehicles are used throughout the battlefield in such roles as command and control, troop and cargo transport, maintenance, and administrative functions. This vehicle can be employed in all types of Army missions, including territorial defence, domestic emergencies, and overseas operations.
MMA	Multi-mission Maritime Aircraft
MOC	Military Occupation Classification
NATO	North Atlantic Treaty Organization: a military and political alliance created in 1949 to maintain stability in Western Europe and deter a Soviet attack during the Cold War. It has since evolved into a method of maintaining European stability in the Stabilization Campaign.
NCM	Non-Commissioned Member
NDHQ	National Defence Headquarters
NORAD	North American Aerospace Defence Command: established in 1958, NORAD is a bi-lateral Canadian-American command designed to deter, detect, and counter an air or space attack against North America.
O&M	Operations and Maintenance
QL	Qualification level
RA	Realty assets, such as offices, hangars, warehouses
retd	Retired
ROTP	Regular Officer Training Plan
SCONDVA	Standing Committee on National Defence and Veterans Affairs
SELEX	Submarine Life Extension
SIGINT	Signals Intelligence: the collection of transmitted information for analysis and exploitation.
SLEP	Service Life Extension Programme

STRATCOM	United States Strategic Command
Tac Hel	Tactical helicopter
TAS	Total Authorized Strength
TCCCS	The Tactical Command and Control Communications System
TEE	Trained Effective Establishment
TES	Trained Effective Strength
TOS	Terms of Service
TPS	Total Paid Strength
UASTAS	Unmanned Aerial Surveillance Target Acquisition System
WSSP	Weapon System Support Plan
YOS	Years of Service

Queen's Policy Studies
Recent Publications

The Queen's Policy Studies Series is dedicated to the exploration of major policy issues that confront governments in Canada and other western nations. McGill-Queen's University Press is the exclusive world representative and distributor of books in the series.

School of Policy Studies

Campaigns for International Security: Canada's Defence Policy at the Turn of the Century, Douglas L. Bland and Sean M. Maloney, 2004
Paper ISBN 0-88911-962-7 Cloth 0-88911-964-3

Understanding Innovation in Canadian Industry, Fred Gault (ed.), 2003
Paper ISBN 1-55339-030-X Cloth ISBN 1-55339-031-8

Delicate Dances: Public Policy and the Nonprofit Sector, Kathy L. Brock (ed.), 2003
Paper ISBN 0-88911-953-8 Cloth ISBN 0-88911-955-4

Beyond the National Divide: Regional Dimensions of Industrial Relations, Mark Thompson, Joseph B. Rose and Anthony E. Smith (eds.), 2003
Paper ISBN 0-88911-963-5 Cloth ISBN 0-88911-965-1

The Nonprofit Sector in Interesting Times: Case Studies in a Changing Sector,
Kathy L. Brock and Keith G. Banting (eds.), 2003
Paper ISBN 0-88911-941-4 Cloth ISBN 0-88911-943-0

Clusters Old and New: The Transition to a Knowledge Economy in Canada's Regions,
David A. Wolfe (ed.), 2003   Paper ISBN 0-88911-959-7 Cloth ISBN 0-88911-961-9

The e-Connected World: Risks and Opportunities, Stephen Coleman (ed.), 2003
Paper ISBN 0-88911-945-7 Cloth ISBN 0-88911-947-3

Knowledge, Clusters and Regional Innovation: Economic Development in Canada, J. Adam Holbrook and David A. Wolfe (eds.), 2002
Paper ISBN 0-88911-919-8 Cloth ISBN 0-88911-917-1

Lessons of Everyday Law/Le droit du quotidien, Roderick Alexander Macdonald, 2002
Paper ISBN 0-88911-915-5 Cloth ISBN 0-88911-913-9

Improving Connections Between Governments and Nonprofit and Voluntary Organizations: Public Policy and the Third Sector, Kathy L. Brock (ed.), 2002
Paper ISBN 0-88911-899-X Cloth ISBN 0-88911-907-4

Institute of Intergovernmental Relations

Federalism and Labour Market Policy: Comparing Different Governance and Employment Strategies, Alain Noël (ed.), 2004
Paper ISBN 1-55339-006-7 Cloth ISBN 1-55339-007-5

The Impact of Global and Regional Integration on Federal Systems: A Comparative Analysis, Harvey Lazar, Hamish Telford and Ronald L. Watts (eds.), 2003
Paper ISBN 1-55339-002-4 Cloth ISBN 1-55339-003-2

Canada: The State of the Federation 2001, vol. 15, *Canadian Political Culture(s) in Transition,* Hamish Telford and Harvey Lazar (eds.), 2002
Paper ISBN 0-88911-863-9 Cloth ISBN 0-88911-851-5

Federalism, Democracy and Disability Policy in Canada, Alan Puttee (ed.), 2002
Paper ISBN 0-88911-855-8 Cloth ISBN 1-55339-001-6, ISBN 0-88911-845-0 (set)

Comparaison des régimes fédéraux, 2ᵉ éd., Ronald L. Watts, 2002
ISBN 1-55339-005-9

Health Policy and Federalism: A Comparative Perspective on Multi-Level Governance, Keith G. Banting and Stan Corbett (eds.), 2001
Paper ISBN 0-88911-859-0 Cloth ISBN 1-55339-000-8, ISBN 0-88911-845-0 (set)

Disability and Federalism: Comparing Different Approaches to Full Participation, David Cameron and Fraser Valentine (eds.), 2001
Paper ISBN 0-88911-857-4 Cloth ISBN 0-88911-867-1, ISBN 0-88911-845-0 (set)

Federalism, Democracy and Health Policy in Canada, Duane Adams (ed.), 2001
Paper ISBN 0-88911-853-1 Cloth ISBN 0-88911-865-5, ISBN 0-88911-845-0 (set)

John Deutsch Institute for the Study of Economic Policy

Canadian Immigration Policy for the 21st Century, Charles M. Beach, Alan G. Green and Jeffrey G. Reitz (eds.), 2003   Paper ISBN 0-88911-954-6 Cloth ISBN 0-88911-952-X

Framing Financial Structure in an Information Environment, Thomas J. Courchene and Edwin H. Neave (eds.), Policy Forum Series no. 38, 2003
Paper ISBN 0-88911-950-3 Cloth ISBN 0-88911-948-1

Towards Evidence-Based Policy for Canadian Education/Vers des politiques canadiennes d'éducation fondées sur la recherche, Patrice de Broucker and/et Arthur Sweetman (eds./dirs.), 2002 Paper ISBN 0-88911-946-5 Cloth ISBN 0-88911-944-9

Money, Markets and Mobility: Celebrating the Ideas of Robert A. Mundell, Nobel Laureate in Economic Sciences, Thomas J. Courchene (ed.), 2002
Paper ISBN 0-88911-820-5 Cloth ISBN 0-88911-818-3

The State of Economics in Canada: Festschrift in Honour of David Slater, Patrick Grady and Andrew Sharpe (eds.), 2001
Paper ISBN 0-88911-942-2 Cloth ISBN 0-88911-940-6

The 2000 Federal Budget: Retrospect and Prospect, Paul A.R. Hobson and Thomas A. Wilson (eds.), Policy Forum Series no. 37, 2001
Paper ISBN 0-88911-816-7 Cloth ISBN 0-88911-814-0

Available from: McGill-Queen's University Press
c/o Georgetown Terminal Warehouses
34 Armstrong Avenue
Georgetown, Ontario L7G 4R9
Tel: (877) 864-8477
Fax: (877) 864-4272
E-mail: orders@gtwcanada.com